AF479956

FLOWATREE

COLORFUL JOURNEYS

OF A BUTTAFLY

Taushae Barber

"I BEAR WITNESS THAT NO READINGS IS GREATER THAN THE READING OF THE WORD OF THE GOD. LORD HELP ME TO UNDERSTAND YOUR WILL FOR MY LIFE. HELP ME NOT TO FORGET THAT YOU PLACED ME IN ALL MY SEASONS FOR A PURPOSE. HELP ME TO SEEK YOUR FACE DAILY AS YOU ORDER THE STEPS IN MY LIFE. IN JESUS CHRIST NAME I PRAY. AMEN"

Dedication

I dedicate this book to my beautiful daughters, Branae Landon, Akilah Buchanan, and every princess who dreams of becoming a strong, powerful, successful queen.

Acknowledgment

Special thank you to the amazing women who raised me. To my grandmothers, Clara and Edith; to my wonderful mother, Tracy; to my beautiful aunties, Terry, Tina, Becky, Susan, Peaches, Shirley, Pill, Gene, Cindy, Lori, Chrystal, and Angie (and many more beautiful women I forgot to mention). Thank you to my daddy, Jimmie; your First Lady did it. I know you want me to hit the stage, taking over and touring throughout countries. After reading this book, I bet you will be just as proud of me. To my stepfather, James Dade Sr., may you rise in power; God bless the heavens. I know you wanted nothing but the best for me, and for that, I will make sure that your children and grandchildren experience the life you wanted them to have. Thank you to all my grandfathers and uncles; your mentality of a rich man helped me to think like a free woman. To the rest of my bloodline and close friends, y'all already know; if not, thank you too.

Contents

Preface

Peace be onto the Creator of the heavens and the earth. We are still here; glory be to God. My crown and cross are still blessed, and I'm trying my hardest not to stress. I don't sweat the smalls; I just keep on balling. Every day is Father's and Mother's Day. I am so blessed and proud to say I enjoy creating colorful wealth for my family. The education, music, books, sports, scripts, and projects I commit to are rewarding avenues. Exploring roadmaps towards scholarships, grants, pensions for children, and families of color is an act of service that I do honor. I want to thank all supporters and a special God bless for the Butta love if we have ever crossed paths. I will continue the work of building, creating, and helping to establish platforms toward positive growth. God, I ask of you to keep like-minded people around me and mine. Wealthy folks who can and will advise, help, support, and endorse dreams, ideas, and goals. Actions speak louder than words. Lord, I'm tired of falling for bullshit. I pray for romance, loyalty, and gifts. I want to be showered with an abundance of true love. My beautiful God, I know you have great plans for me as I do for myself. I will continue to exercise my confidence, wisdom, and overall beauty while I safely educate myself and others on these colorful journeys. I wish us nothing but the best, love, peace, and soul. New Buttafly doors and more is what I thank the Lord for.

"I know trouble is here, but all things are going to work out in my favor. Behold, God is my helper; the Lord is with them that uphold my soul. I always win. I don't know how He does it, but I trust in God, AMEN". ~

After carefully reading the opening statement of each chapter, ***try experiencing my poetry with Afro beats or some instrumental sounds****, you might just catch a whole new wave.*

You can also take these poems and claim that number one spot at spoken word or open mic night.

Recite *them out loud at game night, and* ***watch*** *how they add character and confidence to anyone with a voice.*

Now let's go! ***Flow and grow****, and don't forget to* ***share your videos****.*

1

ATTACHE'

Thank you, Lord, for the betterment of society. The improvement of human and social conditions is building our strengths and creating much better results in the world. Local and international improvements are being done by communities, where everyone is blessed in their own skill set. Focusing on strengths and possibilities is helping us recognize that we are experts in our own situations. When young adults are exposed to principles of human equality, freedom, and democracy throughout their education, it is more likely that they will be protected and responsive to issues of racism and authoritarian state behavior. We need and will get more support for the diplomats with special responsibilities in the culture. Look how great God is; there are people of all colors out here creating social change. Can you believe that there are Afro-Americans studying economic development more than ever before? I see more children of color gaining self-empowerment by scrutinizing imperfect leaders of society. Showcasing the abilities of our colorful power is driving more economic opportunities to the communities that need it the most. The National Urban League, one of America's oldest civil rights organizations, focused on "enabling people of color to secure economic self-reliance, parity power, and human rights." Culture attaché is a term that is used in education, business, government, and academic research. It is maximizing intellectual achievements. When we start making sense of foreign ideas and blending experiences where moments of greatness are realized, those roads more so will keep us on the paths to sweet victory. I would like to ask all readers, what does the H.R.4 mean to you? "Our blessings are not the blessings of a day, a week, a month, a year; it is a blessing of a lifetime." And I remixed a quote from the great John R. Lewis.

MAN THIS LIFE IS HIP TO BE.

GOTTA FREAK IT, ITS SOME REAL WOMEN NEXT TO ME.

I GOTTA KEEP IT, BECAUSE THE LOVE SEES THE BEST IN SHE.

I GO THE HARDEST AND THE BEAT SETS MY SPIRIT FREE.

BETTER STOP, LOOK AND LISTEN BEFORE YOU CROSS THE STREETS.

LOVE THE YOUNG KINGS AND QUEENS HOOD CELEBRITIES.

HIGH NOON, I'M JUST ROLLING WHERE THE BETTER BE.

YOU WANT TO SPOON?

I'M CHILI WITH THE LEFT EYE SPEECH.

DIG THIS I'M EARTHA KITT, A GOLD GRAND MARKI.

BUT I AM NOT WITH THE SHITS I NEED TO SEE ID.

NO MORE GETTING PISSED BECAUSE WE ALL GOING TO EAT.

I'M JUST MEETING MY STATUS OF LIBERTY.

DELIBERATELY IN THE MIDDLE OF LITTLE DIDDLY,

DIDDLING WITH A PENN STABILITY.

I MEAN PENN STATE.

FLOWATREE

COLORFUL JOURNEYS OF A BUTTAFLY

SAY SAY WITH THE CHEESE FACE.

HONDA PILOT LONDON UNDERGROUND BRIEFCASE.

I WAS ONCE LOST NOW I'M FOUND WITH THE KEEPSAKES.

QUEEN, I'LL BOW DOWN AND BLOW A ROUND WITH YOUR BEEF CAKES.

I CAN NOT, YES I CAN, I SOCK NINES IN SOCCER VANS.

I GET MINE AND GODS PLAN.

A MILLION ACRES AND A RAM.

TO BUILD MY KIDS A FIELD OF SAND.

CASTLES, PRIVATE BEACHES, HORSEBACK RIDING LASSOS.

THEY CAN NOT SNEAK DIS.

DO WHAT YOU WHAT BUT WATCH OUR SPEAKERS.

I STAY OUT OF THAT LANE WHERE TALK IS CHEAPER. ~

HI, BYE CENTENNIAL, NATURAL.

I BUY STRAIGHT FACTS IF YOU SELL THEM.

I RIDE IN THE BACK WITH SOME BELLS ON.

FIRST YOU HAVE TO SWEAR TO GOD YOU WON'T TELL ON ME.

I CAN READ AND WRITE BETTER THAN A CELL DORMY.

MAD SCIENCE TRIPS, MAE JEMISON SOARING.

PULL UP WITH THE STICK, SPARK FIRE WHILE IT'S STORMING.

RICH GLITCH SO THE MONEY KEEP ON FALLING.

MIGHT LOAN YOU A YARD, CUT MY GRASS IN THE MORNING.

SHABOOGIE SHABAZZ PUT THE X IN THE O'N.

REAL FIRST CLASS FROM JETSON TO JONESING.

TUCK MY SWAG BUT I WALK LIKE I OWN IT.

WHEN ITS MINE PLEASE BELIEVE WHERE ITS GOING.

OLD MONEY SO YOUNG MY KIDS KEEP ON STORING.

BANK ON THAT, NEW SCHOOL IN THE BACK.

THEY WANT THIS, PLUS GOT MC AND MAC.

SO I HAD TO, REALLY DO THIS AND THAT.

AND WE CAN'T STOP NOW, NO WE WON'T LOOK BACK.

I'MA HIP AWAY IF YOU NEED TO HOP.

I'M A GRIP TODAY MY FIST TO BALD TO SNAP.

THIS WRIST TO RAW TO RAP.

BETTER CHART THIS AUTOGRAPH.

RETHINK THE THOUGHTS YOU HAD.

THINK INSIDE THIS BAG. ~

EVERYTHING HIGH END, FACE DOWN RIDING.

THE WRONG HOE, I'M SELLING IF YOU BUYING.

STRAIGHT DROP FROM THE EARTH.

A NATIVE I DID IT FIRST.

POCAHONTAS HALF BLACK.

I'MA RUN IT, YOU RUN IT BACK.

POKER FACE, I NEVER FOLD.

I'M BEAUTY IN THE BEAST MODE.

A BORN LEADER DIAMOND CUT EAST COAST.

THINK YOU GRILLING WITH MY OLD MEAT RE POST.

GUESS WHAT YO?

JOKE ON YOU, FOOLS GOLD.

I BLESSED HIM THO, BUT NOW I'M THRU.

NO VEGETABLES IN MY CHINESE FOOD.

FLOWATREE

COLORFUL JOURNEYS OF A BUTTAFLY

I'M NEXT TO BLOW THE LINES I MOVE.

A DECIMAL COMMA, COMMA CREW.

HE SAID IMU, I SAID I AM ME TOO.

FORWARD SLASH, BACKSPACE WON'T DO.

DOUBLE CLICK THE SHIFT, SHE MIGHT TYPE TOO.

I DELETE SOME PICS, THEN QUICK TO SKYPE BOO.

MAC BOOK TOO MACINTOSH, CYBER SURF A MINAJ.

CAPS LOCKS ON ALL PROBS, COMMAND ON ALL KNOBS.

COMPUTER LOVE, I SOCKET TOO PLUGS.

COMPUTER LOVE, MY DELL RICHER THEN S. JOBS.

I KEEP BOUNCING ON DESKTOPS.

SEARCH ENGINE I CAN'T STOP.

NO GLITCH, NO COMPLAINTS.

GATEWAY IF THE SYSTEM THE SAME.

DON'T MAKE MY ICLOUD RAIN.

C.O WRIST TUNNEL THE LANES.

I'M A SITE, I SOAR WHENEVER DATA AIN'T RIGHT.

EXPLORE THE WEB LIKE A SPIDER MIGHT.

MEGABYTES SCREEN SWIPE CURSE EM OUT UP AND RIGHT. ~

NEW BARS NEW LIQUOR BETTER FIGURES.

THAT'S WHY I PRAY FOR ALL RICHER NIGGAS.

I PAVE ANY LANE THAT THE SHOVEL DIG US.

THAT NEW FRONT BACK, PINIFEL GLIFFEL.

NEW ON TRACK, SORRY FOR THE SWIVELS.

TRYING TO DRIVE STRAIGHT BUT I'M A LITTLE DRIZZLE.

FOR SHIZZLE MY NIZZLE.

Taushae

STILL ON PIZZLE, OR A PUZZLE?

JUST A FIGURE, I FIGURE THAT I LOVE YOU.

I'M ON THAT AND I AIN'T NEVER GOING BACK.

SO HIGH MY BODY, MIND, SPIRIT IS ON STACKS.

I BE RIDING BY VIA CADILLAC.

I STAY WAVY SO THANKS FOR THE HI'S BACK.

THANKS FOR THE RIDE BACK.

THANKS FOR THE RIDE LADY.

BLACK TOPS, NEW GILLS, HI BYE BABY.

I'M ON A NEW DEAL, I LOVE YOU, PAY ME.

BEEF A TWO PIECE, MASH POT AND GRAVY.

I DON'T LET THE BS FAZE ME.

CAPITALIZING ON THE DAILY.

CRACKING A SMILE, YOU SO CRAZY!

I'M WILD N OUT, HONEY MAYBE.

STYLING WITH A FEW LADIES.

I AM A CEO, ONE HUNDRED THOUSAND DOLLAR PAGES.

I CAN WRITE FROM WRONG AND THEY CAN NOT ERASE IT.

I HEARD IT IN YOUR SONG AND YOU ARE FAR FROM BASIC.

SWEAR TO GOD.

SO JUST SING ALONG, GRACE ALONE IS AMAZING.

SOUL TRAIN SAVING.

I GOT A TRACK RIDING, EVERYDAY WE GOING TO MAKE IT.

I KEEP SOME EARLY FOR THAT LATENESS.

JUST STAY G GLORY AND RE PRAY MISS.

YOU CAN GET YOUR LIFE BACK, JUST REPLAY THIS.

CATCH ME IN THAT WHITE MARSAI SIS, DOING A DANISH.

FLOWATREE

COLORFUL JOURNEYS OF A BUTTAFLY

LEGENDARY OOPS IS MY SECONDARY LANGUAGE.

I JUST PRESS REBUKE, I AIN'T MESSING WITH NO LAMENESS.

HIGHLY SKILLED IN WHIPPING FOREIGNS.

WE DON'T DRIVE THE SAME STICK.

SAME NEWS, DIFF SCHOOLS, REAL BOOBS!

NO HOMO BUT WHAT'S THE DEAL, DOUGH?

ALL IN FROM MY KNEES TOO MY AFRO.

I MIGHT SEND IF YOU BETTER THAN THE LAST BRO.

DON'T MAKE ME UNMASK YOU, GET BACK BOO. ~

LIVING PROOF PULL UP IN A GHOST.

CANDY PAINTING BUTTAFLY SOULS.

A REAL ESTATE, INVESTING IN MY FLOW.

SUPER CORPORATE STRONG A LISTIC ZONE.

FROM PENN AVE TO LIV POPE IN ROME.

I BEEN BAD, I MIKE JACK THE WRONGS.

DOUBLE BACK TO RETRACT MY CALMS.

I'MA MASTER MOM.

A MASTERMIND WITH A DIVINE TWINE.

I GET HIS AND MINE, ALWAYS IN THE SHINE.

I'M FROM HIS RIB, SO I COULD NEVER BE DENIED.

I AM HIS CHILD, THE APPLE OF HIS EYE.

HE IS MY EVERLASTING FATHER,

A WONDERFUL COUNSELOR IN TIMES. ~

LOYAL TO THAT G GLORY.

TUNE UP TRUE STORY.

FROM MY HOOD TO WHO'S WORRIES?

BIG WORLD KEEP ON TURNING.

GLASS HALF FULL, F IT KEEP POURING.

BARS BYPASS ALL THE BORING WHORING.

WONDER WHY THEY CALL YOU BISH?

BECAUSE YOU TWERK TO THAT SHIT!

ME TOO ON THE LOW BUT BRO I GOT KIDS.

SO RESPECT MY FLOW WHEN I DO MY THANG THANG.

I CAN SEE IT IN YOUR RICE CHICKEN WING.

YOU DA GOT DAMN TRUTH LIKE THE BLACK J.B.

I BE SHOOTING FROM THE SIDE, I BOUGHT BACK THE THREE.

I'M ON MICHELLE NUMBER EIGHT, IT'S D'USSE AND B.

THROW EM BACK WE GOT EM WATCHING MAC AND ME.

P.A. ROCK THE BELLS, LADIES LOVE YOURSELF.

I'M FROM THE CAP WITH NO CAP AND I WEAR IT WELL.

SAME ROAD DIFFERENT TRACK, I'M BACK DOING DEALS.

SO QUICK WITH IT AND THEN I MAKE A SALE.

SO MUCH COMMISSION IN THIS PIMPING I COULD KISS AND TELL.

YOU SLIPPING IF YOU TRIPPING, THINKING I MIGHT FAIL.

HOLY WATER ALL ABOUT IT, F THEY DRY ASS WELL.

NO VASELINE F THEY DRY ASS WELL.

THIS IS ALL SPIT, DON'T TAKE IT PERSONAL.

YOU ROCKING WITH THE REALEST WHO YA CHAUFFEUR NOW?

FLOWATREE

COLORFUL JOURNEYS OF A BUTTAFLY

I BE AT THE SHOW GETTING LOVE FROM THE CROWD.

PAGEANTS ON THE WEEKEND, I'M TRYING TO HOLD IT DOWN.

FLIRTY THIRTIES STILL THUGGIN, SHRUGGING THROUGH THE TOWNS.

BOX DOZENS AND SQUARED UP WITH MY ROUNDS.

WHO'S THE JOKE NOW?

POP UPS, COUSIN PETE POUNDS.

IT'S GOLD IN THAT BEAT BROWN, SELL IT TO THE CLOWNS.

GOTTA MOVE YA FEET AND WALK IT OUT.

SHUCK, JIVE, CLUTCH IN DRIVE, PLAN A, I'M PULLING OUT.

NO LAZY BOY OR POTATO HEAD ON MY COUCH.

I'M WAVY NOW. SURFBOARD WIPEOUT'S.

NO BAD ENERGY, THE LIGHTS OUT.

STILL HIGH AS ALMIGHTY ON MY CLOUD.

I AM A BARBER SO CUT IT OUT.

GOOD WITH THE WRIST, FINGER ROLL WITHOUT A DOUBT.

TAKE ME ANYWHERE BUT YOU WILL NEVER TAKE THE GOD OUT.

I CLEANED PLATES UP NORTH AND DID DA DIRTY IN THE DIRTY SOUTH. ~

I KEEP IT PUSHING LIKE SPINDERELLA.

GROOVING, YEA I'M GROOVY.

WHY THEY SALTY, I JUST WIN A STELLAR.

MOVING TO MY OWN ONE TWO, ONE TWO.

STEPPING IN THE NAME OF LOVE.

REALLY SOCK IT TO THEM PLUGS.

MOONWALKING ON L.E.D. RUGS.

FEELING GOOD AND GIVING HUGS.

NEVER LATE, I WILL NOT DEBATE.

I WONT BE MAD SO FIX YA FACE.

LIFE IS NOT SHORT, LIVE IT TO THE FULLEST.

CLEAN AIR STAIR STRAIGHT, BE A GOOD SPORT.

TRYING TO FIX MY CITIES MINORITY REPORT.

HAD TO SWITCH MY TEAM TO THE BLACK WINNING STORKS.

GOT US ALL CLEAR JERSEYS,

GOT MYSELF LIL THIRSTY.

ANDY PALMER I NEED A ARNOLD PALMER RED BULL AND SOME VODKA.

A SUPERLEGGERA TO SPIN THE MOUNTAINS AND GET SOME TOP AH BLOCKA.

HEY KIDS TONIGHT'S DINNER IS JIMMIES MOM STOVE TOP.

PINEAPPLE VEGGIES BEANS AND FRIED TURKEY CHOPS.

BBW'S LOVE TO SWITCH TOO.

I NEED SOME PURPLE SWISS JUICE.

TOO WASH DOWN WHAT'S THE ISSUE.

HE SHE WITH THE TISSUE.

JUST KEEP STUNTING UNTIL THEY MISS YOU.

LET THEM KNOW WHERE THEY CAN KISS YOU. ~

BLACK GIRL MAGIC, BLACK DADS MATTER.

NEVER SLIPPING, STILL TIPPIN AND NOW I'M WHIPPING FASTER.

ONLY LIGHT STRIPPING, SIDE BOOB ACTION.

IF YOU DON'T WANT DAT PACKAGE

FLOWATREE

COLORFUL JOURNEYS OF A BUTTAFLY
I'LL TELL MY COUSIN TO GRAB IT.

BORICUA, MORENA, GEMELOS TOWER PASSION.

BETTA MAX, BEAMER JETS, I GOT ACTION MR. JACKSON.

WHO GOT NEXT? REP YO SET, HASHING WITH THE TAGGING.

ROLL THE BEST, BUDDAH BLESSED, BABY BELLA RAP
SNACKING.

FROM BOBALOBS TO BRACKETS, BAGGING ALL THAT
PASSION.

MY GOD I BE CAPPING, WEAVING THROUGH THE TRAFFIC.

I'M JUST BLESSED AND BRAGGING ABOUT THIS SISTER
CIRCLE MAGIC.

LIVING MY LIFE LIKE IT'S LAVISH, GOOD LORD I'M GLAD I
IMAGINE. ~

NEW ROUTE ON JACKIE TAN.

ALL MONEY RAPED IN BANDS.

ALWAYS WEAR A RUBBER I CAN'T DO NO MARRIED MAN.

SEE I FALL IN LUST TOO QUICK.

WITH THAT HEAD GAME AND DOPE TRICKS.

THE TYPE OF DUDE HAVE ME WALKING AROUND VAJAYJAY
LIKE A ANALOG STICK.

JESUS SPECIAL TEAM PLAY PICK.

THIS MAN'S LOVE IS ALL UP IN MY HIPS.

BABE ASKED ME FOR A THREE SUM BUT I THINK I CAME TO
QUICK.

MY BAD, I GOT A THING FOR A BOSS CHICK, YEA I LIKE EM
SLICK.

A LITTLE MARY JANE, KK MIXES KEEPING UP WITH KRIS.

I NEED A NICE THICK STRIPPER CHICK WHO POWDER UP HER

LIP.

FLY ME ALL AROUND THE WORLD, SHE BE TAKING ME ON TRIPS.

SHE ALWAYS CALLING ME SIS.

DON'T GET CUTE BECAUSE BOO WILL SHOOT.

I KEEP HER IN MY LEFT TIT, BUTTERFLIES KISSING YOU.

I'M HERE TO PLEASE BACK AT THE RANGE, DIP DRIP SAUCE.

I'M PASSING THE JUICE, PASSING TO COOP, LONG BALLS, BIG BOSS.

FIVE RINGS FIVE STARS, XT5 HOME, HOME PHONES MARZ. ~

2

BUTTAFLY MAGIC

The true Black human resource is our mindset. God, universe, and nature, that is our G.U.N. We've won many wars with this powerful tool. We inherited a protective spirit and sound minds. Did you know we have the power to create vaccinations, gold, diamonds, and natural resources? Liberate yourselves, kings and queens. In doing so, we will continue gaining tools in dismantling systemic racism and serving to close the racial wealth gap. Helping America love women of color again is a debt that should not be hard to pay back. The Higher Education Act is a source of accomplishments and great pride for the African American communities as well as the entire nation. We must continue promoting HBCUs, the students, the scholars, and heritage. I thank God for those who support the communities and the organizations that are conducting studies that protect Black lives, human rights, and freedoms. These are things we all can do to keep this balling rolling. A unity of uplifting our people, that is the power. It is our responsibility for promoting our culture while remembering that God controls the speed of the spin. With the wisdom of God and love for one another, there is no journey too hard or far to travel.

I COULD HAVE BEEN BREONNA TAYLOR, THANK GOD I'M STILL GOOD.

AND NOW IT'S TIME FOR THE GOVERNMENT TO FUND THE HOOD.

EVERY COLOR KID A FREE SCHOLARSHIP.

MOMS AND DADS IN GOD WE TRUST YES DEPOSIT THAT.

AND WE WANT EVERY MOTHA LOVING RIGHT BACK.

WE ARE GOING TO MULTIPLY FOR EVERY TIME A LIFE IS SNATCHED.

WHEN THEY PUSH US WE DOUBLE PUSH BACK.

NEW LAWS, NEW PRESIDENT, NEW BLACK.

JUSTICE FOR THE FLOYD FAMILY, BIG FACTS.

I'M IN THE HOOD A MILLION HOODIES, TRAYVON ON OUR BACKS.

SAY HER NAME, SAY HER NAME, SANDRA BLAIN.

AHMAUD ARBREY DIDN'T RUN TOO NEVER WALK AGAIN. ~

HAPPY PEOPLE TODAY BLACK FAM.

THANK GOD WE STILL STAND.

STRONG AND TRULY BLESSED WITH PLANS.

OUR LIFE MATTERS, THAT IS A FACT NOT A DEMAND.

BLACK FAM!

TEFLON FLESH AND PURE GOLD SKIN.

WE MUST NURTURE AND WATER US AS MUCH AS WE CAN.

BLACK FAM!

WE WERE BORN RICH, HIGHLY SKILLED IN POWER.

WE MUST ALWAYS LOVE US THROUGH ANY MATTER.

BLACK FAM!

FLOWATREE

COLORFUL JOURNEYS OF A BUTTAFLY

KNOW YOUR WORTH MY G'Z, WE CAN OVERCOME ADVERSITY.

BLACK FAM!

WE WILL END RACIAL INEQUITY.

DRIVE TO BLACK WALL STREET AND PARK AT LONGEVITY.

BLACK FAM!

DON'T BE AFRAID TO ASK GOD FOR HELP.

BE BLESSED AND PLAY THE ROYAL HAND THAT WAS DEALT.

BLACK FAM! DONT STRESS.

BLACK FAM! IS THE BEST.

BLACK FAM! EQUALS SUCCESS. ~

I JUST NEED A COUPLE BANDS FOR THE WALK THROUGH.

I AIN'T TALKING HBCUS, BUT I BE TALKING TO HBCUS.

BATTLING WITH THE BEST, YES SO COME THROUGH.

WE KEEP THAT GAME ON GO, WHOOTY WHO.

YEA LAST NAME FIRST, WHO IS YOU?

I BE WITH THE OG BEAUTIFUL.

ALL THAT FAVOR ALL OVER ME THANKS TO MY BOO.

LONDON FOG BUT NOW I SEE DIVISION TOO.

I'M THE BOSS I'M CLOCKING IN MY WORK BOOTS.

I GOT THAT PURPLE, I GOT THAT GREEN, I WANT THAT EARTH BLUE.

MELLOW YELLOW FOR THE GEEKS GO BIG URKEL.

GO BIG URKEL, GO GO GO BIG URKEL.

PASS IT TO MY SIS THEN WIGGLE IN A CIRCLE.

KNOWING WHERE MY HELP COMES FROM, HOW CAN I HELP YOU?

OR BETTER YET GO READ A BOOK AND JUST BE HELPFUL. ~

I GOTTA TRUST THE PROCESS. I'M ADDICTED TO PROGRESS.

LIP GLOSS, MASCARA THUGGIN NO STYLIST.

LIPS TAKING SHOTS?

I'M BREATHING FIRE BALL MOUNTAINS.

SURROGATE HOT SPITTA WITH BIG MOUTH TALENT.

PUT THE MILLIONS IN MY HANDS, IT'S MY MONEY I'LL COUNT IT.

KEEP THE FUTURE IN MY PLANS, I WON IT BEFORE I FOUND IT.

GOTTA THANK THE MAN THAT MADE ME.

MY MOM DUKES TO, SHE FOREVER BE MY LADY.

WE GOT THEM FALLING OUT THE SKY LIKE THEY TASTY.

NO MORE CANCER IN OUR BODIES.

BLESS THE QUEEN WITH THE PASTRIES.

I STILL GO DUMB, BLACK GIRL WITH NO PAYSHES.

I GOT PATIENT'S, MY BRANDY BUNCH IS WAITING.

THURGOOD MARSHALL, I'M AT MARSHALLS IN A MATRIX.

RONDO WITH THE LEFT WE LEAVE THE FIGHTING FOR THE PAVEMENT.

I'M GOOD ON ANY BRIDGE AND BOROUGH IT CAN'T CAVE IN.

SO HOOD HBG, THE REAL BURG SUN WAS RAISED IN.

I AM THAT HOLLA BACK AT YA GIRL SIS.

I BE CARPOOLING JUST TO MAKE A WORLD WISH.

IF I'M SWIMMING WITH THE LEMONS, I'M WINNING WINING AND DINING.

EX HOES KEEP ON CALLING JUST TELL MY MOMMY I'M SHINING.

FLOWATREE

COLORFUL JOURNEYS OF A BUTTAFLY

NOISE FOLKS STAY MIND IN, FEET FIRST THEY LYING.

F THE PUMPS WE JUMP HURDLES AT MY END.

SO WHATS SUP WHO GOT ANSWERS?

MY HOMIES BE BUYING.

I SPEAK UP IF YOU HEAR ME I SWEAR TO GOD I'M TRYING.

PRAY TO GOD WHEN I'M RHYMING, RIGHT BETWEEN ALL THE LIONS.

ALTHEA GOLF CART FOR THE KIDS TO RIDE IN.

I GOT A MEAN SWING AND I AIN'T EVEN FIGHTING.

THIS HERE A COOL BREEZE I'M JUST POWER GLIDING.

SPENDING HOURS POWER PRIDING.

THIS G STUFF I CAN'T DENY IT.

GETTING TO IT IN A HYBRID.

MAJOR MOVES FLIPPING MY GIFTS.

I THANK GOD I CAN'T STOP IT.~

I'M STILL FLY AF, SOUL PLANE.

CONNECTING DOTS SO MY CHAIN BLINGS.

MY PHONE RINGS, THEN PLANS CHANGE.

I JUST KEEP DOING MY DAMN THING.

I WON'T TWEET WHAT MY BIRDS SING.

MY SOUL FOR REAL WITH THAT CANDY RAIN.

I SMOKE HEAVY D GOOD GOD SHAME.

LIKE WITHERSPOON, I BANG BANG.

TARGA TOPS AND SPINNING GRILLS.

I THROW IT BACK I'M BLESSED STILL.

BANANA CLIP WHEN I SPIT.

I GO APE SHIT. NO CHILL.

I AM THAT BLACK GIRL IN PLEASANTVILLE.

CHEESY DRAKE FACE ALL THROUGH THE HILLS.

MY VALLEY DEEP, AIN'T NOTHING SWEET.

I'M IN THE COMMONWEALTH AND I NEED MILLS.

I DON'T NEED THIS, I JUST WANT THAT.

I NEVER JUMP SHIP, I JUST RUN TRACK.

I WENT UNDERGROUND AND I TRACED MAPS.

MY GPS IT GETS PAID STACKS.

I PUSH A BUTTON MY MONEY GOING CRAZY, SPIRIT TAKE ME WHERE THAT SAFE AT.

THEN I WAKE UP LIKE WHAT THE WHAT AND THANK GOD THAT I MADE IT BACK.

BECAUSE WITH OR WITHOUT MY SISTERS MY TITTIES UP AND I'M GETTING RACKS.

TOOK MY TIME WITH MY TAKE OFF BECAUSE IT'S POWER IN WORDS I MIGHT TAKE BACK.

I WON'T FLOOD THE STREETS WITH NO BS.

DON'T TAKE THAT THAT AIN'T RAP!

IT'S TIME WE RISE THE UP UP.

DEM BLACK DEMS, DEM TAKE BACK. ~

ON MY WAY TO FORBES, SHOW ME WHAT THAT LIST DO.

A MASTER JACKER.

TIGER IN A JACKET WITH THE WRIST MOVES.

NO DISRESPECT, BUT I CAN MAKE THE MS GROOVE.

WALKMAN FROM CASSETTES TO MY TUNES.

POSTERS! KIDS ON THE BLOCK IN MY ROOM.

FLOWATREE

COLORFUL JOURNEYS OF A BUTTAFLY

ALL MONEY IN THEM STOCKS AND BONDS I WANT THEM.

ALWAYS RUN A MARATHON TO THE END.

IF YOU DON'T SIDE WITH THE FINISH,

IT'S BECAUSE YOU STARTED THE WIN.

BLIND SIDE FROM THE CEILINGS, WILL HAVE YOU WIPING YA EYES AGAIN.

GOD FORGIVE THE WILLING. I DO REPENT.

FALL THRU GOOD TIMES, SO HEAVEN SENT.

IF IT AIN'T ME, HOPE THAT GRASS GET GREEN AGAIN.

SAVE YOU A LONG TRIP, LISTEN TO FRIEND.

BESTIES AND YA EXES, LESSONS LEARNED AND LENT.

PICK IT UP. PICK YA POCKETS BEFORE THEY SPENT.

IF THEY PICK UP ON YOUR DRIP THEY BE BACK AGAIN.

GOT TO HIT THEM WITH FINESSE AND MAKE THEM EFFIN SPEND.

GET DOWN AND FOLLOW.

LAME CRACKERS SWALLOW.

HAD THE BADDEST CHICK, MONICA I KNOW.

JUST KEEP YA HEAD UP MS THING HITTING THEM HIGH NOTES.

SO GONE IS THE REALEST LAME, SKIT I WROTE.

CHECKING ON MY QUEENS WHEN I COPE.

GO ON AHEAD CRY A RIVER, I'LL STROKE, STAIR OR PADDLE.

THE SAME BOAT, REALLY MATTERS.

I TUNE UP AND LET THEM TELEVISE THEY OWN DISASTERS.

I WANT THAT EGOT, FLIP MY SCRIPT, I'M CASTING.

SHOULD HAVE NEVER PLAYED YASELF NOW I'M BACK TO ACTING.

BACK TO CLAPPING, I SURE MISS TWERKING.

YOU WHAT TO BE WITH THEM HOES?

THEN GET BACK TO JERKING.

THREE SNAPS AND A TWIST NOW I'M BACK TO SERVING.

UP THAT GOOD DRIZZY, GOD'S PLAN OUR PURPOSE.

JUSTICE WITH THE BOX BRAIDS, MAXED OUT AND LOCKED IT.

KEYS AROUND MY NECK THE WAR IS DONE I ROCKED IT.

NOSE UP IN THE COCKPIT.

I CAN COACH A FLY CHICK.

COACH HANDED ME THE PLAY BOOK ON A BI WEEK.

LEADER OF THE TEAM RIGHT BESIDE ME.

WORKING ON THAT CHIP, I'M NEEDED WHERE I BE. ~

TO ALL THE LISTENERS WHO BLESSED TO WITNESS, A SOUND SO PROFOUND I HYDRO LIPPED IT.

INFATUATED WITH THE FACT THAT EVIL NO LONGER LIVES HERE.

HI TO THE POLO BEAR I'M ROLLING OFF OF BLANK STARES.

I'M STEPPING UP I OWN MY MASTERS.

CLIMBING WHAT THEY CAPTURE.

I'M A RENEGADE MOMMA MADE CAUGHT IN A RAPTURE.

FOR THE LOVE OF MONEY FEELING LIKE A SELFISH BASTARD.

CAN'T TAKE NOTHING FROM ME BECAUSE THEM THINGS WILL GO BLACKA.

SILLY WONKA, HER SHAE KISSES TO THE DOCTOR.

I'M A GREAT LUCK I GOT THE PUCK UP IN MY POCKET.

ALL THE BOOKS I READ HELP ME SEE THAT I CAN'T STOP IT.

THE C.O.D AND EXCHANGING OF STOCKS.

FLOWATREE

COLORFUL JOURNEYS OF A BUTTAFLY

I GOT A RINGER ON TOP.

WHO TEACH KINGS HOW TO CROSS WHEN THEY BUILDING UP BLOCKS.

I'LL LEARN YOU HOW TO FLOSS AND MAKE A CHAIR OUT OF ROCKS.

NEVER DID THANK MY PARENTS FOR THE TIME THAT I LOST.

I WROTE THE PRESI JUST TO TELL THAT NINJA I AM A BOSS.

IN MY OWN INNUENDO, WALLS AND WINDOWS.

WITH THE WEIRDOS, BUNDLES, BABIES AND SHERO'S.

COMPLAINING THEN EXPLAINING, I CAN'T PASS A DEAL UP THIS COLD.

ROCKAFELLAED MY WAY TO YMCM BEAST MODE.

GET AWAY WITH MURDER WATCHING ABC HOE.

YEAH I DID THE DIRTY BUT THEY'LL NEVER GET MY CHEAT CODE.

LOOKING TO HARD, I'LL LEAVE YOU LOOKING LIKE A PEEP HOLE.

HEY LOVE LET'S SPREAD ONE FOR MY PEOPLES.

POUR A LITTLE LIQUOR NO LYE AND JUNGLE JUICE.

THE GIRL SHAE BUTTA GOT A PROBLEM SHE JUST BLESSED THE BOOTH.

FAIRY TALES OF THE GOLDEN TRUTH.

SMILING ALL THE WAY UP TO THE MAC.

SWIPING LIKE A MACHINE WITH A CHIP ON ITS BACK.

I STILL DO MY LITTLE LEAN WHEN I'M RIDING IN A LAC.

WORKING, WINNING AND WHIPPING UP A NEW PACK.

MY BABE SMIRKING AND GRINNING BECAUSE HE KNOW I'M ALL THAT

AND A BAG A CHIPS BRO.

MADE IT TO THE WHITE HOUSE AND I DID NOT SHOW A NIPPLE.

VALEDICTORIAN AND COLLEGE CREDENTIALS.

I AM NEVER BORING.

JUST GOOD FOR THE MENTAL. ~

BOO BOO I WALK THRU IN THEM BLUE BOTTOM JIMMY CHOOS.

I PAY MY DUES AND HOMAGE TO, TO THE REAL FOLKS WHO BE BUSTIN LOOSE.

I FEEL LIKE BUSTIN TOO.

I FEEL GOOD HOOTIE HOO.

AMONGST MASTER PEOPLE, GREATNESS IS MY EQUAL.

BUTTAFLY LIKE AN EAGLE.

I'M SO RICH ROYAL AND REGAL.

I'M THAT QUEEN ON POINT LIKE A NEEDLE.

I MIGHT WHAT YOU BAD BUT DON'T NEED YOU.

NEVER STINGY, I'M STILL GOING TO FEED YOU BOO.

I BREAK BREAD LIKE JESUS DO.

AND BLEED RED DAMN SO DO YOU.

I WILL PHOTOBOMB YOUR PHOTO SHOOT.

GET THE PICTURE SMILE AIN'T WE CUTE?

I'M FISHING NOW FOR REAL PROOF.

REEL THEM IN AND GRIND THEM UP.

SWITCHING GEARS LIKE A MACK TRUCK.

ALL MONEY IN, I'M GOING UP.

I'M THE BEST IN HERE AND CAN'T STOP.

GOING TO TAKE THIS YEAR AND ONE.

FLOWATREE

COLORFUL JOURNEYS OF A BUTTAFLY

TOP THE CHARTS LIKE DAMN SON.

GET IT BOY. YOU GO GIRL.

OMG MY WHOLE FAM WON.

WHAT YOU THINK I SMOKE FOR?

GOOD LOOKING LIKE A AND ONE.

FROM LONG DISTANCE IMA PASS IT TO MY GRANDSONS.

I'LL PASS OFF IF YOU HANDSOME.

TIP TOEING OVER BREAD CRUMBS. ~

READY OR NOT BUTTA'S HERE.

BLESS YO FEELINGS FACTS MY DEAR.

I'M SPREADING AROUND REAL LOVE FAR AND NEAR.

ALMOST CRIED A RIVER PUSHING MY TOP TIER.

ANOTHER LESSON CREATED, YES I PASSED IT.

MAKE IT FEEL SO GOOD, EVERLASTING.

I'M JUST RIDING THIS BEAT, WRITING ANOTHER CLASSIC.

THEY SAY ONE IN A MILLION, DID HE TWO STEP PASS ME?

I CAN'T LIE YOU REMIND ME OF HAPPY.

LOVE IS ALL WE NEED, I LET THE BULLSHIT PASS ME.

I NEED MORE WEED, BAMBU AND A GLASS PLEASE.

I I CAPTAIN ANOTHER QUEEN TO DO THE NASTY.

"I WANT TO BE DOWN".

I STICK AROUND IF YOU ASK ME.

I GRADUATED WITH THE REALEST AND THE CLASSY.

I'M GLAD YOU MADE IT TO MY FEELINGS, F THAT DAY FROM LAST WEEK.

NEW ACCOUNT AT THE BANK, I LOVE TO SAY CASH THESE.

I MOVE WITH A NEW YORK SPEED, A P.A. PACE.

DO DO BROWN, DC, POLLY YA POCKET FACE.

COME TO YOUR SENSES AND STOP THE HATE RACE.

WON'T GET THE PEOPLES VOTE UNTIL WE ARE ALL SAFE.

BLACK ON BLACK NIGHTLINE WHO DA F YOU THANK?

PACE WITH THE PATIENCE.

DRIP DRIP ON A DAYBED, ALL LEGS IN.

LEGS UP ON A SLEIGH BED, YES I SLAY THEM.

KISS AND DON'T TELL AT THE HILTON NOT THE DAYS INN.

MISS ME WITH THE BS MY BOSS MAN FADE IN.

ONLY TIME I LOSE IS WHEN I'M REALLY NOT PLAYING.

TEAM SKIN, LIGHT OR DARK I'M JUST SAYING.

UNTIL THE END OF TIME MAKAVELI WINGS FLAMING.

FLYING SKY HIGH, I AM AN ANGLE ON THE PAVEMENT.

I LET ANDY PALMER, ASTON MARTIN, I'M AMAZING.

AT YOUR OWN RISK WHEN YOU CLOSE TO MY WAVE.

URSHER JON AND LUDA HAD TO DO IT TODAY, SHIT!

I GOT TOO MANY LOVERS AND FRIENDS THAT I PLAY WITH.

WE GOT IT COVERED PICTURE PERFECT FRONT PAGES.

GOOD NEWS, BIG GIFTS, TAKING OVER STAGES.

SO ENGAGED WITH THE GAUGES.

SHOTTI LOUD AS A PARADE MAN.

RIDING DOWN KNOCKING PICTURES OFF THE WALL, FRAME IT.

ME LLAMO ES NO NAME.

STRAIGHT TO THE POINT CAN'T BLAME THIS.

SAME CHICK ROCKING THE LATEST CHANGING FACES.

FLOWATREE

COLORFUL JOURNEYS OF A BUTTAFLY

WRIST WHIP GRIP, I'M CHANGING LANGUAGE. ~

THERE I GO AGAIN, LYRICAL TESTAMON.

MONIE IN THE MIDDLE, RING UP OR EVERY MAN.

DOUBLE DUTCH, FIRST AND LAST, FIND AND SMASH.

THOSE WERE THE TIMES WE CANNOT LET PASS.

BEFORE APPLE AND IBM BIT OUR SWAG.

TECH, TEK, TEC BLACK GREEN RED FLAG.

KNOWLEDGE OLOGY IN MY WORLD LAB.

TRANSFORM A PUNCH BUGGY INTO A PECAN JAG.

TELL MY DAUGHTERS WORK SMART AIN'T NOTHING YOU CAN'T HAVE.

IN YA MIND IF YOU ARE FIRST I'MA CATCH UP FAST.

SWIM HOMIE, SWIM AND DON'T LOOK BACK.

ON MY SON DON'T NEED A GUN, I'LL STILL BUST THEY ASS.

HE HE HELL THAT WAS A GOOD ONE, ALMOST HAD ME.

CAN'T PLAY ME ZADDY.

YOU GOT TOO MANY WHIPS AND TOO MANY ADDYS.

I'M ON A DESERT WITH A DESSERT CAKED UP LIKE PATTI.

I CLAP ALONG BECAUSE I AM HAPPY.

JOHN JACOB JINGLEHEIMER SMITH AT THE WEST INN.

OR OFF DOING SPLITS WITH MY BEST FRIEND.

HOPPED THE FENCE, IT'S A PARTY EVERY WEEKEND.

BLACK MAGIC BLACK GIRL MAGIC LET IT SINK IN.~

EVEN IF I AIN'T ON THE LIST I'MA STILL MAKE YA VISIT.

PETTY VIOLATIONS, FAKE CHARGES, THEY AIN'T STICKING.

OUR HOUSE WE BUILT IS WAY BIGGER.

THE BLOOD IN OUR LOVE WAY THICKER.

WE SEPARATED YOU STILL MY NIGGAS.

IF THEY HATING THEY DON'T NEED TO GET THE PICTURE.

I DO THIS HERE SO OUR KIDS CAN BE RICHER.

I GOT THE GIFT TO GAB, GOD GOD GIVING.

WE GOING TO MAKE A WAY GOD GOD WILLING!

AS LONG AS EVERYDAY WE WAKE UP WINNING.

IMA KEEP IT REAL FOR MY H-TOWN WOMEN.

WHO IS HOLDING IT DOWN RAISING A VILLAGE.

SO FABULOUS GIRL WE BE KILLING IT.

LIKE HARRIET, CORETTA OR THE VIVIAN'S.

PUT A RING ON IT, HONEYMOON CARIBBEANS.

SHOOTER SHOOTER LEFT HAND VERA WANG.

IN CUBA VACAING JR PLANS, SUN AND SANDS.~

3

SASHAE'

Make me over, Lord. The softness of glorifying our womanhood. In the New International Version, 1 Corinthians 11:15 of the Holy Bible reads, "But if a woman has long hair, it is her glory? For long hair is given to her as a covering." Amen. Black Girl Magic, did you know that Africa matters when finding your way through this beauty world? I thank God for all-natural shea butter. Be proud of yourself, ladies. "Real hair, I do care. Walk like a styllionaire. Leap of faith, F fear, billion-dollar deal, come here." I thank God for the new growth and for the beautiful baby hairs. Yes, edges on fleek! I pray that God continues to allow the hair from our heads to grow so long down our backs. Full heads of healthy hair. Hair from our roots to Africa, so curly, shiny, strong, with unbelievable strengths and unimaginable lengths. Our culture is crowded with beautiful twists, dreads, waves, locks, volume, colors, braids, and many styles, with protection from heat, damage, breakage, and split ends. The hair from our roots, by God, will grow from our great-great-grandparents to our great-great-grandchildren. We can always grow healthy hair. The CROWN Act is a law that was enacted in 2019, creating a respectful and open world for natural hair. This law is successful when it comes to ensuring protection and ending hair discrimination. Our skin is beautiful, but our hair makes us different, so keep it pretty.

I BOUGHT ME AND ALL OF MY MISSES.

CONJUGAL BLESSINGS AT EVERY VISIT.

TOP OF THE TOTEM, WE DON'T MISS SIS.

GOT THESE SKILLS FROM GRANDMA'S KITCHEN.

WAY TOO REAL ABOUT TO START PIMPING.

MADE MY OWN DEAL AND NOW I'M SEEING MILLIONS.

TRIED TO FADE THE BLACK GIRL BUT I AM STILL RESILIENT.

YEA SUMMER IS HOT AS PISS BUT I STAY CHILLING.

I STAY OUT OF MY FEELINGS.

SMILING PROUD TO THE CEILINGS.

WITH MY FAM ON MY SIDE, PARADISE IS THE VISION.

ROLLING RIGHT WITH THE DIGITS.

LOVING LIFE BECAUSE IT'S VIVID.

IF I SAID IT THEN I MEANT IT, BUTTAFLY CAN YOU DIG IT.~

WALK IT LIKE I TALK IT.

BARELY WALKING I JUST PARKED IT.

GLOSSY SMOOCHERS THEY STAY ZIPPED,

I OPEN UP A BIT TO SPARK IT.

I ALWAYS FINISH WHAT I STARTED.

A HIT MAKER HITTING TARGETS.

GETTING LOVE AT THE PARTY.

IS THAT YOUR WIFE OOPS I'M SORRY.

WE BLACK GIRL ROCK AND I GAVE HER BACK.

FLOWATREE

COLORFUL JOURNEYS OF A BUTTAFLY

I'M LIBERTY BELLA RINGS AND RACKS.

I'M WITH THE FELLAS AND THE DIVAS WHERE THAT
GETTING GOOD IS AT.

AMONGST THESE QUEENS I RUN LAPS.

CORNY BEEFS AND PRETTY TRACKS.

DIDN'T SWING BUT DROPPED A HIT, I PICKED IT UP AND
PUT IT BACK.

BOTTOM SHELF FLOW IS A NO-NO.

IT'S JUST ME MYSELF AND DOLO.

I'M ON MY LIBRA SHIT, DEDICATION SIX, A SEAT BELT
HIGHWAY HYDRO.

FAST LANE SWERVING TO GET MY DOUGH.

PSYCHO PMS WHEN I FLOW.

THE CITY ASKING WHERE DID I GO?

I'M AN ICON, A WILD IDLE.

MRS SMITH, JADEN, WILLOW.

I CARRY BAGS BIG AS PILLOWS.

TRENDING LIGHTLY IN MY STEEL TOES.

SLEEPY GARDEN IS WHERE I WAKE THOSE.

BLOOD DIAMONDS, RUBY'S, CRYSTALS.

BRUSH MY HAIR SO BEAUTY BLISSFUL.

RENOVATE TO FIX MY ISSUES, SO SIMPLE.

BECAUSE, I WALK IT LIKE I SPIT IT.

I LOVE RIHANNA WITH THE TITTIES.

MISS ANITA WHEN I BAKE UP.

I'MA SHAKE IT UNTIL THEY WAKE UP.

PRETTY HOES FIX Y'ALL MAKEUP.

I AIN'T PLAYIN WITH NO SEGA'S,

ALL ABOARD ON THIS SAGA.

SAVE THE DRAMA FOR YO MOMMA. ~

THEY TRIED TO STEAL BLACK GIRL MAGIC STUFF, IT AIN'T HAPPENING.

THERE ARE CENTURIES OF QUEENS WHO ARE PREPARED FOR THE CAPPIN.

THEY TRIED TO STEAL BLACK GIRL MAGIC SWAG, NO SIR.

I ADVISE YOU NOT TO TOUCH MY PURSE.

THEY TRIED TO STEAL BLACK GIRL MAGIC PEACE, NEGATIVE.

SEE, GOD HAS WORD FOR MY LIFE AND MY LIFE IS IN HIS WORD.

SO IF I DIG DEEPER WITH HIM THERE IS NO ROOM FOR ABSURD.

NO TIME FOR COMPLAINING AND NAGGING, NOT SHE.

ONLY TEARS OF JOY ON MY FACE WILL YOU SEE.

BECAUSE I LEAN ON HIM AND NOT ON ME.

WITH WORTHSHIP, REPENTANCE AND GLORY TO THEE.

HE PICKS MY CROWN OFF THE GROUND AS I BOW TO MY KNEES.

THANK YOU MY KING, SO THANKFUL I BE.

HE IS STRONG WHEN I AM WEAK AND THROUGH HIS STRENGTH, I'M BACK UP IN THIS PEACE.

YES, THANK YOU, I THANK YOU, I THANK YOU MY

COLORFUL JOURNEYS OF A BUTTAFLY
LORD. ~

I GOT THAT MILLION DOLLAR TONGUE I DON'T TALK TOO MUCH.

 BUT WHEN YOUR FINGER SO TRIGGER A GOOD POINT WRITES TRUST.

I BLAST OFF NOT KIRKO.

HOT POTATO WITH MY CIRCLE.

HOOD DICTIONARY, DODGEBALL THE FAKE NEWS.

WINDSTARS TO WINSLOW'S.

WE NEED MORE LAURA'S AND URKEL'S.

BLACK LAWYERS, DOCTORS AND COMMERCIALS.

I BE THAT RICH BLACK GIRL WITH A PURPOSE.

OVERCOMING ARTIFICIAL, DON'T MAKE ME NERVOUS.

BABY LOVE AND BABY HAIR QUEEN D ANNA.

I AM A BOSS DOUBLE MG'z, NO HANDS IN THE LAMBO.

MOUTH FULL OF THAT TWENTY TWO AMMO.

SUCH A SIN TO WASTE I BE LIKE DAMN YO.

WHEN I'M ON DUTY I'M A PERFECT EXAMPLE.

CLOCK WORK ON RUDY, I CLOCK OUT LIKE PAM THO.

GOT IT DOWN PAT I'M IN THE DAMN ZONE.

WET WET LIKE CANCUN SCOOP YOU A SAMPLE.

SAM I AM. I AM TOO. HOT DAMN I'M SO DAMN COOL. ~

SORRY FOR THE DELAY. I FORGET I GOT STUFF TO SAY. I WAS OUT OF CHARACTER IN THIS PLAY.

ROLL CALL I'M HERE TO STAY.

STAY WET SO GIVE A F ABOUT A RAINY DAY.

I BET ALL MONEY IN THE WOOD WAY.

I'M GOOD BAE TO ALL MY HOES.

MY ROUNDS KNOW, IT'S A CIRCLE OF LIFE.

PICK YA PRICE, PREMEDICATE, DON'T THINK TWICE.

ELEVATE, LEVEL IN, AND MAKE THINGS NICE.

WHY NOT BLING ICE?

PATIENCE WILL BUILD PIPES.

PRESSURE BUST OFF RIGHT.

THE BASTERS BETTER NOT MIGHT!

I'M FASTER THAN THE SOUND OF LIGHT.

THUNDER CAT, BULL DOGGING WITH BIKES.

BARK FULL OF ALL BITE.

YOU GOING TO LEARN TODAY I'M ALRIGHT, ALRIGHT, ALRIGHT.

AT MY OWN WHERE I STAY.

HOW YOU HERE WITH NO INVITE?

NOT TALKING OFF WHITE.

BROWN LIQ FOR THE NIGHT.

ME CASA MY OWN SITE.

BOOGLE ON A DRUNK NIGHT.

AQUA FLOW I KEEP IT TIGHT. ~

FLOWATREE

COLORFUL JOURNEYS OF A BUTTAFLY

I'VE BEEN GONE FOR A MINUTE.

NOW I'M BACK JUST TO JUMP IN.

I'M NOT FROM THE N SO Y THE F THEY KEEP GASSING?

SOLAR POWER, ME AND MY SON, FLEW PAST WIN.

FINISH LINE WE WON, OUR SNEAKS SNUCK IN.

PAT ONE AND TURN THE OTHER, MY CHEEKS CHECK CHINS.

BIG BEEF WITH THE RUBBER, I SKEET PAST THEM.

BIG BUTT BABY MOTHER, I COULD HAVE SMASH.

BUT I LEFT HER UP TO YOU LIKE THE LAST ONE.

PLAY BEAUTY SMART, ON THE LOW I HEARD SHE MAD FUN.

THAT SO AND SO AND SOME TO NONE MAYBE BIG PUN.

NO PUN INTENDED UNLESS ITS COMING FROM A REAL ONE.

YOU CAME IN IT WITH THEM THICK THIGHS, SIS RUN!

WHEN YOU PAUSE FOR THE CAUSE YOU BETTER BREAK SOMETHING.

BARRIERS AND THEM STALLS, DON'T PISS OFF THE PUBLIC!

I SPIT AWFUL LOVELLETTE.

I LOVE TO TURN ON THAT OFF SHIT.

WHO WOULD KNOW THOSE CARTIER BRACELETS ALL FIT.

HAD TO LET IT BURN WHEN I HEARD THAT THE SOURCE SNITCH.

STITCHING ALL I EARNED, KUT KLOSE SCAR CLICK.

WOMB TO WOMB MARK IT, DOCTOR JUNIOR MARTIN.

FROM WAKANDA TO SPARTAN, SEE MONEY ALL IN.

THE SUN SET HERE WEST COAST IS CALLING.

SUNRISE ON THE SHAW, EAST COAST IS BALLIN.

MIDDLEMAN TELL MONIE SHE'S A DARLING.

BIGGER LAND, WE PART TREES AND THE PARTRIDGE. ~

MY LORD PUT ME IN POSITION, OMG FINGER LICKING.

MY WINS THEY'RE NEVER ENDING.

THAT WHITE GOLD WHIPPING.

I'M NITRO WHO IS THE GLYCERIN?

WHEN I FLOW YOU SHOULD LISTEN.

I'M ON GO I'MA KICK IT.

ALWAYS GREAT IN MY KITCHEN.

SELF CLEAN MONEY RINSING.

MELTING DRIP FOLLOW THE DRIPPING.

CHECKMATE PUT THE TIP IN.

CHESS TO CHESS WITH ALL HIS WOMEN.

LIVING SINGLE MAX TO THE CEILINGS.

CAP OR CROWN F THEY FEELINGS.

ROOT CANAL OCEAN SAILING.

SCUBA DOWN MIGHT CATCH THE TAIL END.

MOMMY SHARK FROM HERE TO WHELAN.

GOOD AND WOKE WHO YOU ALEING?

NO MO WAITING TO INHALE IT.

COLORFUL JOURNEYS OF A BUTTAFLY
SHOOTING SHIT WITH THE PALET.

SO HIGH I MEAN PILOT.

BUILD IT UP THEY WILL BUY IT.

HOME PLATE SLIDING.

STRAWBERRIES AND HIGH PITCH.

CUP YOUR NUTS, DON'T LET THEY JOCK YOUR
JOCKAGE.

IF YOU LET THEM IN THEY WILL SAY YOUR OUT OF
POCKET.

JUST KEEP WINNING THEY CAN'T STOP IT.~

STRAIGHT OUT OF BOMPTON.

GOD STILL BLESSING TEAM SHAE.

HIGH TOP LIKE KID ROLL PLAY.

WIN, WIN I STAY DRAWING BOTH WAYS.

BLACK EASTER HAPPY HOLLY BOTH DAYS.

I'M BACK FLYING HEALTHY HAIR, CROCHETS.

DREAD SHIT I GOT IT LOCKED GATES EIGHTY EIGHT.

OH MY GOD I JUST WANT TO WIN THE DAY AWAY.

MAKE LOVE TO A SUNNY RAY JUST ME MONEY AND
BAE.

STREET QUEENS, I'M A QUEEN IN THE STREETS I PLAY.

MASK ON OR OFF, I WILL SHACK ATTACK IN THEY
FACE.

BLESS UP, POWER PUFF, BLACK POWER WHAT THE
BUCKS.

WE MAKING MAGIC IN THIS WORLD, WISH YOU THE

BEST OF LUCK.

YEA I TRAVEL FOR THE GIFTS SO GIVE IT UP.

SUCH A LOVELY LADY AND SUCH I GIVE HIM LOVE.

HENNY WINGS AND THINGS, GOOD LICKING
FINGERHUT.

SEXY SEXY YUP YUP DOING THE BUTT. ~

I KEEP IT SO SIMPLE, SENSITIVE NIPPLES.

THE BEST YOU KNOW POPPING LIKE DIMPLES.

GUCCI WITH THE LOCK, CHANDLER OUT THE BOX.

ENERGIZER HONEY I BE TWERKING OUT MY SOCKS.

AIN'T NO CRYING IN BLACK BALL.

SWITCH WHEN I WALK TALL.

SEE A GLITCH AND I TAKE OFF.

MASK UP THEN I MAKE OFF.

F WHAT IT MAY COST.

I SPEND A DAY ON THEY'RE CAUSE.

H. BERRY I'M JUST DOING THE RAY CHARLES.

NO HABLO CAN'T HEAR LAW.

I'M KILLIN THIS DANCE OFF.

HAMMER TIME WHEN MY PANTS OFF.

REALLY NOT HARD THEY JUST TOO DAMN SOFT.

ON GOD WE WILL CONQUER AND WIN ALL.

DOWN WITH THE SQUAD THEN I AM UP LIKE
HANDBALL.

I'M WITH THE PODS, PEAS AND CAN GOODS.

COLORFUL JOURNEYS OF A BUTTAFLY

MY JOB IS TO KEEP IT REAL HOOD.

FINESSING THAT POSTA SHOULD.

BLESSING THEM ENGINES THAT COULD.

WE THE BEST YOU UNDERSTOOD? ~

RUB B.U.T.T.A ALL IN

TOASTER IN THE HOLSTER PROTECT YA SKIN.

I GOT KISSES FOR THEM WISHES BLOWING IN THE WIN.

I KEEP LOVING ON YA MISSES THRU THICK AND THIN.

I AGALAPIZE IF YOU OOPS TASTE MY GIN.

ODD SQUAD I AIN'T EVEN WANT TO LET YOU IN.

BLACK GIRL MAGIC, GOOD LORD FORGOT I HAD IT.

PMS TO TSA WATCH WHO THE F YOU GRABBING?

FOR WHAT REASON, I'M ASKING?

LITTLE LOOSE LIPS, WET GLOSS MACKIN.

TALK A MILE A MINUTE, I GET PAID FOR YAPPING.

FOR REAL DOUGH, WORD UP STACKING.

SEMI AUTO AD LIBS, SCRIBBLE, SCRABBLE, SCRAPPING.

VOCABULARY TACTICS, HIBBIDY HABITS.

POTENTIAL IN CREDENTIALS GLOBE TROTTING
CLASSIC.

IT'S JUST FUNDAMENTAL.

IT'S JUST FUN TO MEND TWO.

IT'S JUST FUN TO MEN TOO.

NOW WATCH WHAT YA GIRL DO.

IN THAT PRESIDENTIAL, WITH BULLET PROOF

WINDOWS.

STOCKS IN THEM GEMS AND BELLA JEWELS. ~

AIN'T NO NEED TO FAKE THE FUNK, YOUR BEST BET IS TO TELL THE TRUTH.

YOU KNOW I ALREADY HAVE THE PROOF.

YOU KEEP SLEEPING ON A QUEEN, I NEED A STAND UP DUDE.

STILL LYING AND SHIT, LIKE DAMN WHAT I DO?

GOT ME BUYING BS LIKE A GODDAMN FOOL.

BUT I'M NOT INTO TURNING TRICKS INTO HOLLYWOOD HUBBY'S.

I GET BACK ON MY GRIND, SHINING BRIGHT I KNOW I LOVE ME.

I DON'T PLAY WRONG WAY AND THAT'S HOW YOU RUB ME.

GOT ENOUGH LONG DAYS, I HAVE NO BUSINESS CUFFING.

YET WE BOTH GROWN AND YOU TOO OLD FOR THE BLUFFING.

I KNOW THE BRO CODE, "G'D UP, F HOES GET MONEY'.

BUT WHEN THAT B ROLL TOUCH MY TOES, GOT DAMN I'M RUNNING.

GOOD GIRL TURN AND TELL THE BADDIES I'M COMING.

AHH WHAT YOU THOUGHT YOU WAS LOVING A DUMMY.

ALL THE HEAD THAT YOU GOT YOU SHOULD HAVE LEARNED SOMETHING FROM ME.

FLOWATREE

COLORFUL JOURNEYS OF A BUTTAFLY

I AM NOT GOING TO DRAWL, I'MA LET IT BURN UNTIL YOU EARN IT.

I'M GOING TO PLAY THE BLOCK WHILE YOU CHASING A LITTLE DIRTY.

F 12, I PLAY THIRTY. ~

4

BUTTA LOVE

The Lord's covenant reads, "I am the Lord your God, who rescued you from the land of Egypt, the place of your slavery. You must not have any other gods but me. You must not make for yourself an idol of any kind, or an image of anything in the heavens or on the earth or in the sea. You must not bow down to them or worship them, for I the Lord your God, am a jealous God who will not tolerate your affection for any other gods." Amen! Butta love is truly from the heart. I love the Lord with all my heart and soul. I know that key time with God is important. That is why I seek Him first as soon as I awake and accept His way of doing things for me. The blessings of the Lord make a place rich, and for that, I will lean on my love for His wisdom and grace. It's such a good look when more corporate companies are offering expert-guided resources of interest to those who want to become self-sufficient. Multi-talented leaders have been conducting studies that protect our colorful journeys. When we begin to blend progressive attention to evaluate our history, the practices are protecting and valuing the lives of our youth. Some messengers preach the method of using instruments of love to build a nation. I agree that spreading the education of consulting and coaching is principal for wealth gaining. This is why we must continue to spread love by honoring our transformative

COLORFUL JOURNEYS OF A BUTTAFLY

figures all around the world and supporting the gathering of educators. Staying in front of the struggle will create jobs to help end all poverty and want. Raising the value of Black lives by offering high-end guidelines to access financial capital is a great covenant to a successful world. Never forget, "we are generational wealth".

MY VIBRATIONS ARE LOVE, LIFE AND LIBERATION'S.

REPARATIONS I FIGHT FOR WITH NO HESITATIONS.

WE BUILT THIS LAND, STRATEGICALLY WITH AMAZING GRACES.

I'M IN THIS JAM, BELIEVE ME AND WE GOING PLACES.

THANK YOU BIG BRO, THANK YOU SISTER SOLDIER GIRLS.

A HUNDRED MORE I SWEAR, I SWEAR WE CAN RULE THE WORLD.

EXOTIC TRIPS, US IN THE SIX.

EVERY OTHER PRETTY FLICKS.

TAKING OFF GIVE ME THE WHIP, WE BLACK RICH.

FRONT BACK FLIPS. I'M BACK BISH, SOLDIER SACK SHIT.

THEN I PASS IT. FILL EM UP, MY GAS LIT, ON LITTY.

TURNING UP THE WHOLE CITY, TEN O'CLOCK BIG TITTIES.

I PROMISE WE WILL GET IT, ON GOD, RIP BLACK ROB. ~

IT'S BEEN A MINUTE SINCE I HAD A CRUSH BABE.

SO PLEASE FORGIVE ME IF I FALL THRU A MINUTE LATE.

STRAIGHT OUT THE PEN, BANGOLA I GOT A RICH MAN.

HE DID ME SO GOOD I SEE HIM IN MY FUTURE PLANS.

THE LONG D GIVE A LIFT, I'M FEELING ON MYSELF.

BEEN A BAD GIRL TOO LONG, MY LORD, GET THE BELT.

BETTER YET GET THE RING AND SOME ANGELS TO SING.

IT MIGHT BE OVER HASKA DA MEAN.

TRIPS TO ANYWHERE, EATING GOOD, BIG TINGS.

TOLD THEM MY GOODIES FULL OF GOLD, I CAN ONLY BLESS KINGS.

PURPLE RAIN THIS IS WHAT IT SOUNDS LIKE WHEN DOVES BLING.

CROSSED THE OCEANS, CLIMB MOUNTAINS OLD AS YAO MING.

EXCUSE MY BRAGGING, WET DREAMS GOT ME BUSSIN BUSSIN.

FIRST SIGHT FLIGHT, ON THE PIPE, I THINK I LOVE HIM.

BE CAREFUL FOR WHAT YOU ASK FOR, QUESTIONS KEEP THEM COMING.

UNTIL THE BIG ONE POP, KEEP IT ON THE LOW IN THE OVEN. ~

LOOKING FOR MY HUBBY FEELING BIRTHDAY CRAZY.

IN MY DRAWS AND JORDANS COWGIRL TAKE ME.

SOLIDITY FLASHING TITTIES, TAKE OFF FOR MY CITY.

FLOWATREE

COLORFUL JOURNEYS OF A BUTTAFLY

VEST ON ME, STRAIGHT SHOT WHEN I PRAY FOR THIS MILLY.

THE BEST OF ME THEY WILL NEVER GET, DIDDLEY, DIDDLEY.

I GOT THE STEM TO FREEZE A MELTING POT SILLY BILLY.

I GOT JEANS ANYWHERE I ROCK LIKE UNCLE WILLY.

AMBLE~ENO AMA` AMA`, THEN I AM BACK NEXT TO PHILLY.

I REALLY DO GET AROUND KID YOU NOT LIKE GILLIE.

STATE PROP ISLAND WHEN THEM STACKS IS HEAVY.

MIGHT DROP A COUPLE CHINS GET Y'ALL FACES READY.

I GOT THE GAVEL, I GOT THE GAVEL AND I'M NOT AFRAID TO USE IT.

I GOT THE KNOWLEDGE AND THE POWER STACKED UP RUBIK'S.

CERTIFIED A TO Z BECAUSE I DON'T ABUSE IT.~

MOMMA AIN'T RAISE NO HOE.

A LADY IN THE STREETS AND THE REST SHE PRAY FOR.

ELEVATOR HANDS FROM THE SKY TO THE FLOOR.

I THROW IT BACK, LEFT RIGHT CHEEK, DEMOCRATIC POLLS.

I'M THE ONE HE THINKS ABOUT WHEN SHE CAN'T GET IT UP NO MORE.

I BE GAGGING JUST FOR FUN HE REFLEX AND GIVES ME DOUGH.

TEXT HIS GIRL HE BE BACK GRABBING BUTTA AT THE STORE.

MY GOD HURRY UP AND BUY, THINGS TO DO THINGS TO GO.

I'M IN MY FLEX BANGING SWV FEELING LIKE E.V.E.

A BALANCING ACT, SHADY HOES CAN'T SON ME.

MY GRAND MOMMA RAISED A PRO.

SO RUN UP AND GET DONE UP, FREE HANDS FREE SMOKE.

I GOT THAT DIAMOND WRIST THAT TWIST UP LIKE ITS STIR FRY.

PLUCK A CHICKEN HEAD IN HER HEAD, HOE I POP EYES.

GOT WHAT YOU WANT, I KEEP A BAG IN MY TETAS.

MS. PINK, MR. GREEN OR MRS. BLANCA.

DRIVE MS. DAISY NOW I'M WAVY, I THINK I BLEW ABOUT AN EIGHTY.

FEELING LUCKY WHERE IS BABY?

I'MA BLESS HIM AND HIS LADY.

DON'T BE MESSING WITH MY TIME, WOKE BOY WHO YOU PAY ME.

I AIN'T COME TO HERE YOU WINE, I GOT COGNAC AT THE TABLE.

WHO THESE QUEENS ON MY LAP DANCING LIKE I SIGNED A LABEL?

THREE LINES AND MY ADIDAS WEEZY DRAKE SAID HIT THEM ANGLES.

SPREADING BUTTA ON THE TRACK, I KILL THE BEAT THEN SHAKE MY BANGLES.

FLOWATREE

COLORFUL JOURNEYS OF A BUTTAFLY
DON'T KNOW WHY EVERY TIME I SHAKE MY ASS THEY
THROWING SINGLES.

I JUST SHAKE MY HEAD ASS AND ALL.

HE BLEW A KISS I LAUGHED IT OFF.

AIN'T BUY A DRINK BUT HE WAS CUTE SO I GOT HIS
NUMBER AND I AIN'T CALL.

I'M THE SHORT SHIT STILL STANDING DRUNK AF BUT
NEVER FALL.

I'M WINNING COMPS, I STAND AND AIM, YOUNG PODS
PLEASE DON'T SIT AND STALL.

UNLIMITED HOTLINE BLING, A BP CALLING CARD.

EXCUSE ME IF I BUMP A QUEEN I MEANT TO SAY
PARDON DOLL.

DON'T LOSE ME WHEN YOU BANG MY ISH THIS AIN'T
FOR ALL OF Y'ALL.

I'M BOUGIE WHEN IT COMES TO THIS, NO TLC
WATERFALLS.

MILKSHAKES KEEPS ALL THE BOYS SEEING STARS.

HE BRINGS THE D AND I KEEP THE HAAGEN-DAZS.

GOTA HAPPY EVER AFTER AT THE END OF MY
MASSAGE.

LEAVE A HAPPY LUCKY CAMPER, SINGING KUMBAYA.

LEAVE HIS BEARD DRIPPIN, WET YES ALHAMDULILLAH.

NOT DROWNING HE WAS SLIPPING BREAST STROKING
IN MY POND.

I'M THE TYPE OF CHICK TO RUN A TRICK ON MAGIC
DON WON.

ABRACADABRA NOW YOU SEE IT? YES I'M ON. ~

YOU KNOW WHAT TO DO TO MAKE MOMMY A LITTLE WETTER.

TAKE IT BACK LIKE A PERK AND MAKE US FEEL BETTER.

DO WHAT YOU PLEASE WHAT MY BODY BABY I'MMA LET YOU.

I'MA HIT IT THREE TIMES THEN ACT LIKE I AIN'T MET YOU.

DAMN I JUST HAD DEJA VU.

FLASHBACKS OF WHEN I FIRST GAVE IT UP TOO.

THAT DOPE STICK, I SWEAR HE POPPED A LITTLE BLUE.

HE BEAT IT TO THE POINT I SCREAMED I BLOW THE D TO.

I TOOK IT OUT ONE AND PUT IT IN ANOTHER.

THE FIRST TIME I EVER RAN FROM A LOVER.

SIKE, OH MY, THIS STRONG SPIRIT MUTHA BROTHA.

HE HAD ME PRAYING TO THE CEILING,

HAD TO TELL GOD I LOVE HIM.

YEA I LUCKED UP. HE LUCKED UP YOU TO.

DID ME SO GOOD NOW WE STUCK LIKE GLUE.

DON'T BE MAD, BECAUSE I WILL MAKE IT UP SOON.

MATTER FACT I'LL KISS IT FIRST BECAUSE I MISS YOU.

~

FLOWATREE

COLORFUL JOURNEYS OF A BUTTAFLY

I'M BACK AT IT LIKE JESS RABBIT.

BUT I DON'T LAY MY BACKUP ON A CRAFTMATIC.

ME, I'M GOING TO RIDE THE TUNE ALL NIGHT.

SO BUST IT OPEN AND I MIGHT JUST BITE THE PIPE.

HIM, HE GOT MY BREAST SITTING PRETTY YES.

ASK AROUND HOLY GROUNDS AND THE CITY'S BEST!

I GO HAM SLIP AND SLIDING UP AND DOWN THE POLE.

I DON'T STRIP BUT I WILL MAKE THE DOLLARS FLOW.

HOLD UP, I'M MONEY DANCING ON THE BED BABY.

HANDS UP, MILLY ROCKING ON THE COCK CRAZY.

A HALF A GRAM MORE THAT WILL KEEP YA GIRL WAVY.

SPLASH PARTY ALL NIGHT WELCOME TO THE NAVY.

OOOUUU, YOU KNOW YOU ARE "IT" BOO.

AND WHEN YOU MAKE THIS WATERFALL I SALUTE YOU.

YOU HUSTLE REAL HARD AND YOU BRING THAT D TOO.

DON'T LET YOUR WIFE KNOW BUT I'M ABOUT TO WIFE YOU!

WE HAVE TO KEEP IT ON THE LOW PRO.

PRETTY LADIES IN HIS BED HELP MY MOJO.

AND IF SHE BAD SHE CAN JOIN, HOMO.

I TEACH YOU HOW TO KEEP YA MAN PROMO. ~

THESE QUEENS DON'T DO IT LIKE THIS.

I BE SPITTING ON THE MIC AND I DO IT ON THE STICK.

TELLING BEDTIME STORIES I'MA RULER MISS SLICK.

I GOT BOYZ IN THE HOOD, THAT RUN FAST LIKE RICK.

HOLLA FOR A DOLLA, I GOT THAT POWER FIFTY CENT.

I'M SINGING LA LA ON KEY UP IN LA LA LAND.

GLASS FULL LIKE MELO GOTTA STAY ABOVE THE RIM.

RIDE OR DIE FOR MY SQUAD I BE SHOOTING IN THE GYM.

I HAVE A GREAT PRENUP FOR HIM A PLATINUM VISA.

I'M ON, IN THE CLUB HIGH SINGING DEPOSITO.

I GET THAT STRAIGHT DROP FROM MY RICAN NAMED PITO.

SIS WITH THE SIDE EYE SQUINTING YUP ME HOE.

LONG AS GIRAFFE NECK SO I HAD TO DEEPTHROAT.

OPENED THE DOOR, DROPPED A BRICK THEN THE KEY BROKE.

LAME ASS DUDE, THAT'S MY STORY AND I'M STICKING TO IT.

I DON'T LIKE LAMES, THAT'S MY STORY AND I'M STICKING TO IT.

BODAK WE IN ALL BLACK.

WE GETTING MONEY IN THE STREETS WE TAKING ALL THAT.

MAKE IT RAIN IN THE HOOD AND HAVE THEM GIVE IT ALL BLACK.

HOW DOES IT FEEL NOW? CAN'T GET YA BALL BACK.

FLOWATREE

COLORFUL JOURNEYS OF A BUTTAFLY
I'M JOE CLARK WITH THAT BASEBALL BAT.

MY LORD LEAN WITH ME AND THE LEAN ON DECK.

I LIKE MY CUP A COUPLE ROCKS DOUBLE BRANDY OR THE JACK.

NEVER SLIPPING ON MY FACE JUST RELAXING ON MY BACK. ~

I ONLY TAKE EM SWAGGED OUT, NEVER BRAG ABOUT

BUT KEEP A FAST MOUTH.

WE KNOW THAT JOB AIN'T GETTING DONE UNLESS MY G GOT A CASH ROUTE.

DOPE BOY HE KEEP ME ICED. LOYALTY, I'M DOWN FOR LIFE.

WHO ELSE ARE YOU GOING TO CALL TO TAKE THAT PIPE?

A FREAK LIKE ME ALWAYS DOWN TO RIDE.

HASHTAG G CODE, KEEP ME FROM THEM FOES.

RULE ONE TO PAPER CHASING, GO GETTER'S WE NEVER FOLD!

HE'S A HOT BOY, MY KING SPIT THE TRUTH AND I'M THE REALEST.

BEAUTY MET A BEAST, DROP THE BEAT AND THEN WE KILLED IT.

IF YOU LAME, THEN UP OUT MY LANE YEA BOY BYE.

I ONLY PLAY A RUBY SIDE HOE WILL NEVER SLIDE.

HARRISBURG'S BEST SHAEBUTTA BE THE SMOOTHEST.

AS FOR DUDE, IF HE AIN'T OFFICIAL I DON'T DO'S IT DO'S IT.

I STOP DIGGING FOR GOLD, NOW ADDICTED TO HOPE.

IF I DIG HOW YOU ROLL, THEN I MIGHT LET YOU STROKE.

OH YOU A HOT BOY? YOU OWN A BLOCK BOY?

I GOOGLE PEOPLE, SO I HOPE YOU AIN'T A COP BOY?

I KEEP IT THE REALEST, GIVE A F BOUT THEY FEELINGS.

IF I WAS OUT WITH DA BULL, THEN IT IS ALL ABOUT BUSINESS.

HE'S A ROC BOY. HE KEEPS IT IN THE SOCK BOY.

WATCH WHAT YOU SAY BECAUSE HE AIN'T AFRAID TO POP BOY. ~

YOU DON'T THINK I PAY ATTENTION TO THE THINGS YOU DO.

MY MIND, BODY, SPIRIT WAY UP THANKS TO YOU.

ONLY IF YOU KNEW, I BE DAMNED IF I DIDN'T.

NOTICE HOW YA LOVE MAKING KEEP ME SMITING.

I GOT YOU FINGER LICKING.

WINDOW SHOPPING FOR A ROCK TO GET MY FINGER GLISTENING.

LISTEN!

I RECOGNIZE ITS TIME FOR RECOGNITION.

TOLD ALL THE DUDES IN MY INBOX THEY CAN CALL ME MRS.

HOLD UP I JUST GOT A TEXT, OH A COUPLE KISSES.

SO PETTY GOT ME SMILING AT HIS OLD BISHES.

SHAKING MY HEAD AT MY OLD HOES I WON'T MISS

THEM.

FALLING FAST FOR HIS LOVE BABY GOT ME TRIPPING, TRIPPING. ~

HE'S NEVER TO MUCH HE HOLD ME JUST RIGHT.

ALL NIGHT I LET HIM BEAT IT UP WITHOUT A FIGHT.

I'M TALKING HANDS UP EVERY ROUND I'M TIED UP.

UNTIL I CLIMAX, THEN HE LEAVES ME ON LUCK.

FUCK! MY BABY GOT ME GOING AMAZING.

GOT ME SWEATING OUT MY BANGS WHEN I'M SUPPOSED TO BE A LADY.

FUCK, ALL THE LAMES THAT PLAYED ME.

I BOW GRACEFULLY FOR THE WRONGS THAT MADE ME.

SO HD, SO TAKE ME YEAH MAKE ME, YA WIFEY FOR LIFE.

NO SICKNESS JUST HEALTH I LOVE THE WAY HE PIPE.

IF LOVING YOU IS WRONG I DON'T WANT TO BE RIGHT.

JESUS CHRIST I LIKE. HE KISS IT SO GOOD THE PILLOWS I BITE.

WHEN BAE HOME EVERYTHING JUST BRIGHT.

HE LOVES ME SO GOOD, FOR THE RING I MIGHT. ~

HE'S GOING TO HOLD IT DOWN SO I GOTTA KEEP IT UP.

GET THAT ARCH IN MY BACK I CAN FEEL IT IN MY GUT.

MY BABE LONG LEG AND KEEPS HIS BUTTAFLY.

I'M GRIPPING ON THE WOOD HE SLAP A FIVE ON MY THIGH.

HE IS OMG, WHOLE MAN AND SO AMAZING.

I GIVE THAT D BOY A STANDING OVATION.

AS A QUEEN I HAD TO BOW TO HIS GREATNESS.

NO TIME FOR OTHER MEN THEY CAN GET THE WAITLIST.

BUT HE CAN GET THE BAY LIST.

MEANS WHEN YOU WANT IT, YOU CAN TAKE IT.

AND WHEN YOU NEED ME I GOT YOU.

FROM THE BEDROOM TO THE BLOCK BOO.

HIS AND HER SMILEY FACES WHEN WE COME THROUGH.

I'M BANGING MARY "SHARE MY WORLD" IN MY OLD SCHOOL.

BECAUSE LOVE IS ALL WE NEED AND YOU ARE EVERYTHING.

TRUST I CAN'T GET YOU OFF MY MIND.

I'M BITING DOWN ON THESE SHEETS NO I'M NOT GOING TO CRY. ~

MY MOJO BACK, DAGGER ON CHILL.

PANTIES ON DRIP DRIP ALL IN HIS GRILL.

DO IT FOR THE REALEST YOU KNOW I REALLY WILL.

SWINGING WITH A GRIP, LET GO AND EXHALE.

BUTTERFLIES BUTTERFLIES ALL I FEEL.

HE KISS IT SO GOOD, DO I TELL.

DON'T NEED A NAN NOTHER BABY GOT SKILLS.

INFRARED SHOOTER FROM THE BED TO THE FIELD.

FLOWATREE

COLORFUL JOURNEYS OF A BUTTAFLY

I LIKE IT ON TOP. HE CLIMB OUT THE BOX.

I DON'T KNOW WHEN TO STOP, HE MAKES ME SUPER WET.

HE LIKES WINNING BETS. POKE ME TO POKER CHIPS. ~

5

ASHAY

Green morning! It's time to wake and bake. The sun must rise, and we will grind. By the grace of God, we're building economic self-sustainability, positive space making, and creating infrastructure for other successful people. There are multi-millions in revenue for cannabis agriculture. Behold good and pleasant, agriculture analytics determined for farmers of color, there's billions in aid now available. Even non-smokers are successful at growing. Kush College is a green supremacy tech center in the growing field, servicing over thousands who study, focus, and invest in African Americans in the marijuana industry. Social equity in the cannabis industry and the legalization of cannabis on a national level are two of our main focal points. We have access to land assets and land wealth. We are granted mineral rights. Marijuana dispensaries are doubling thanks to the public and charitable funds. Kush College, the Green Supremacy, and the study of social equity in cannabis agriculture, are educating generations of cannabis industry leaders by creating programs, communities, and events. Thanks to those spreading the message using their voices to get the word out about cannabis criminal justice reform. Decriminalizing cannabis is an economic engine for revitalized communities and pathways to peace and prosperity. For a greener tomorrow, we can help by

COLORFUL JOURNEYS OF A BUTTAFLY

signing petitions that demand action, immediate relief, and generated clemency for cannabis prisoners. Emerging bills in the marijuana field will increasingly help the economy, local communities, and the healthcare industry. At Kush College, in God, we grow ownership, create generational wealth, and assets that our families can pass down to our children and grandchildren. These forms of cash, investment funds, stock and bonds, properties or entire companies will be in our families forever more.

I BE OH BLEVEY BE OH BLINDY TO THE STUFF I PUT BEHIND ME.

TO THE PAST I LET INSIDE ME.

TO THAT LAST GOOD LOOKING NINJA I LET WALK BY ME.

TRYING TO FIND ME TO NO CRIMIES.

GOT ADDICTED TO MY SELFIES.

THE POT IS MELTING,

I CAN'T HELP IT BECAUSE I DEALT IT.

REAL HANDS IN HOLLYWOOD.

SHORT ARM, LONG REACH.

ANOINTING THE POINTS WITH THE PREACH.

OH MY JEEZY. NOT A FREEBIE, THIS WILL COST YA.

NOW I'M ASKING WHO YA BOSS HUH?

I AM MISS BARBER NOT TO CUT YA.

FEELING UPPERS, YEPPERS EXCUSE MY FUCKERS WHEN

I'M UPSET.

JESUS, I GOT LOVERS I AIN'T MET YET.

JESUS, I GOT JUGS I AIN'T BUST YET. I GOT BLUNTS ON THE TABLE, PLUS WEED, THE LORD SAVED ME.~

HOLY KISSES TO ALL MY BUTTERCUPS.

I WILL ALWAYS KNUCK IF YOU BUCK.

WE ARE ON THE SIDE WHERE ITS BEST OF LUCK.

SMOKING ON THAT LA LA, I'M TESTING UP.

ARE YOU GOING TO REP OR WHAT?

I'M TRYING TO STRETCH THE LUCK.

ELASTIC THE PLASTIC GOLD MEDAL THE PUMPS.

HITTING SWITCHES FOR THE RICHES I'M CASHES CLUMP.

HOLD YA BRITCHES, REST YOUR JACKETS AND ADDRESS YA WANTS.

OUTFITS OUT NEW LOOKING SO SUPREME.

A ONE LOVELY LADY WITH A SOLDIER LEAN.

ONLY WAY ONE, STRAIGHT UP FOR MY TEAM.

IN ONE DAY WE CAN DO WHAT THEY DREAM.

I'M EAR CHASING THE BLING, I CAN EYEBALL A KING.

SO ATTENTIVE TO REDEMPTION WHEN THEY MENTION MY NAME.

I REALLY HUSTLED THEM LANES, O T TO THE GAME!

LITTLE OH ME IS STILL THE SAME, MORE MONEY AND CHANGE. ~

FLOWATREE

COLORFUL JOURNEYS OF A BUTTAFLY

I DO IT FOR MY G'S WHO STILL BUYING O'S.

ONLY THAT ILL, LEGAL D ROLL AND GO.

I BE LIKE DAMN MY NINJAS, WHERE THE LOVE AT?

THAT'S WHY IT'S HARD TO LEAVE THE BLOCK, I MUG THAT.

BLACK COFFEE, KISS CAFE, GIVING HUGS BACK.

HOW OFTEN DO WE EMBRACE OR GOT OUR BLOODS BACK?

A HEALING FACTOR AS A MATTER OF FACT.

TRAP LORD AND LOCKED DOORS FROM THE FRONT TO THE BACK.

TIME TO EXPLORE THE MOTHERLAND, YES BACK TO THE ROOTS.

RULER OF THE NEW SCHOOL, PLEASE PREACH THE TRUTH.

FREE WORLD, IT'S UP TO US TO PICK AND CHOOSE.

OH BOY, WHO ME GIRL? I DON'T DO THE BLUES.

BEAUTIFUL BLACK BUTTAFLY, REPORTING LIVE FROM MY VIEWS.

WINS BOSS SHIT, TIES AND DO'S.

SHOW Y'ALL WE CAN NEVER LOSE.

I'MA BRING ALL OF ME, JUST BRING ALL OF YOU.

STAY TUNED IN TO LADY SINGS THE COOLS.

SOUL CALL ALL THE WAY TO THE MOON.

MORE ROOMS, SHIPS, CHIPS, EXOTIC TRIPS.

TG4 ALL THE THINGS WE CAN FLIP.

ALL MY PEOPLE GETTING RICH.

NO MORE PLAYS WITH THE STICK.

SO PULL AND CATCH THIS BLICK.

REALLY WITH THE GIFTS, MOVING BOOKS LIKE BRICKS.

RUN THRU TOWNS AND IT STICKS. WE GETTIN IT! ~

I'M GETTING ARAB MONEY, WHAT YOU KNOW ABOUT THAT?

I TIE A RAG AROUND MY HEAD, I'M MISSES I GET RACKS.

NEVER ON NO BROKNESS, SIS I SELL TRACKS.

AND IF YOU AIMING AT MY QUEENS YES I BUST BACK.

REAL RAP, TRILL DIVA, WITH A GANGSTA ASS DEMEANOR.

LET'S GO L FOR L AND I BET YOU MINES IS GREENER.

I HEARD ITS BEEF SO I'M RIDING WITH THAT NINA.

ACTING LIKE ITS SWEET I CAST THEM IN THE SARAFINA.

SO TEAM UP AND GOOD LUCK.

BECAUSE ONCE I SEE YOU ALL SCARY, YOU GET NONE.

NO INTERCOURSE, I'M SHOWING NO REMORSE.

I'M A RICH BISH, I'M NEVER ON THE FRONT PORCH.

I'M IN THE ALLEY DOG GETTING IT F THE LAW.

THE TRAP BOYS IN MY CITY I HELP SUPPLY THEM ALL.

I SWEAR TO GOD I'MA BALL UNTIL I NEVER FALL.

AND INSHALLAH WHEN I GO MY KIDS GET IT ALL.

INSHALLAH WHEN I FLOW MY KIDS WILL GET IT ALL. ~

COLORFUL JOURNEYS OF A BUTTAFLY

SO QUICK TO SAY I'M GOOD BUT THIS AIN'T NO JOKE.

WAS ON A DIET POURING OUT I SUBSTITUTE IT WITH SMOKE.

BAGGED UP NEGATIVITY I KEEP IT PUSHING AND COPE.

I AIN'T AIMING WHEN I SEE DUMB SHIT THRU A SCOPE.

I JUST RAIN MAN, COUNT IT UP THEN I'M BACK TO THE SHOW.

FLIP IT FLIP IT ON YOU REAL QUICK, GIVE ME SOME MO.

LUCKY I AIN'T WEAR MY MASK MAKE YOU GET ON THE FLOOR.

I'M THE MIDDLE OF THE CLASS PROFESSOR OGLEVEE BRO.

AIN'T NO HOLDING ME UNLESS YOU GOT THAT JODECI FLOW.

DOUBLE A SO CHARGED UP AND I STAY ON GO.

NO WAY I AIN'T BUYING SAVE YA SEANCE HOE.

GOLDEN STATE OF MIND TOKING ON THAT DRAYMOND DRO.

RATHER SAVE A LIFE THEN SIT AND BOTTLE UP A FLOW.

ALL THE CAPTAIN CRUNCHING GOTTA GO.

ALL THESE SEXY LADIES ON THE FLOOR.

WYMCMB AND I PUT THAT ON MY BRO.

NINE TWENTY-EIGHT AND I NEED EIGHTY MO. ~

HASTA, HASTA, HASTA MAÑANA.

WATCH YA FACE TIME I SPIT HOTTER THAN A SAUNA.

TELL ME WHAT AND BE KIND WHEN I'M BUYING MARIJUANA.

IF YOU AIN'T INTRIGUE, THIS AIN'T WHAT YOU WANNA.

MY WAY LONG LIKE SLEEVES, WRIST GAME LIKE KAWANA.

SILENCE IS GOLDEN BUT HOES BE TELLING LIKE RWANDA.

I USE A BLACK IRON MAN, JUST TO WRINKLE OUT THE DRAMA.

BACK TO BACK ON JAM, OVER BREAD WHEN I WONDER.

I AM ABOUT THEM STATS, TRIPLE DOUBLES WITH THE NUMBERS.

IF I AIN'T CALL BACK, I DISCONNECT YOUR TELLY TUNNEL.

HI PRITT, HI PRATT, MY ACTIONS IS NEVER UGLY.

I DON'T DIG ALL THAT. I DUG OUT DOING THE DOUGIE.

I SELL LOTS ANYWHERE, ON AND OFF THE RUG B.

GOD IS GOOD ALL THE TIME AND ALL THE TIME YOU WILL SEE.

THAT'S WHERE I GET MY JUICE SO STOP SQUEEZING UP ON ME.

I BE STEPPING OUT ON TWOS ABOUT TO HIT THE

SHUFFLE THREE.

I CAN HUDDLE UP A G.

DON'T MAKE ME CALL THE SPECIAL TEAM.

I USE TO GET THE SIDE EYE, NOW THEY DOING THE

FLOWATREE

COLORFUL JOURNEYS OF A BUTTAFLY

SHOULDER LEAN.

I'M A DREAM QUEEN. I ACT, I RAP, I DANCE AND SING.

WHEN I DO THE DO, I DO THE DAMN THING.

I BE LIKE WHO? WHO GOT TIME FOR THE HATING.

MOVE THEM RIGHT UP OUT MY SPACE JAM.

NOW I HAVE A CLEAR VIEW, WITH NO MORE PATIENCE.

DOCTOR BUTTA PER DIEM.

ALWAYS DOWN TO WORK WITH THEM.

I WAS BORN IN THE GYM.

TIMBER BABY, WIN AND WIN.

LIFE IS CRAZY MADE ME SIN.

I'M WASHING UP ALL THE JINS.

IRK AND JERKING IT AGAIN.

FEW PERKS, JUST TWERKING WITH MY TWIN.

THAT'S LITTLE SIS, REMIXING IS HER GIFT.

REVIEWING THE WHOLE LIST.

REE MURDER IN THIS BISH.

CASHING OUT ON ALL OUR WHIPS.

GOLD BOTTLES AND THE CHRIS.

OLD MODELS DOING FLIPS.

OH IT'S JUST THE BARBERS, CUTTING UP AND OUT WITH GARBAGE.

REAL REAL BIG, YEA WE LIVING PRETTY LARGE MISS.

REALLY GET THEM RACKS FROM TARJAY TO TARGET.

STILL IN THE STREETS ALL BROAD LIKE THE MARKET.

M.L.K. DRIVE IS WHERE I PARK IT.

DON'T MAKE ME SPARK IT, LIKE IT'S 420.

IT GETS DARK QUICK, I KEEP AT LEAST ONE ON ME.

I GO SO HARD, TELL THAT BEAT KEEP HUMMING.

I TEACH YOU HOW TO SHOOT, I'M DR. DRE DRUMMOND.

LIVING PROOF A LITTLE SUMPIN TOO SUMPIN SUMPIN. ~

BUTTAFLY DRO TOO BUTTAFLY DOORS.

WE BE GETTING MONEY AND I'M ABOUT TO GET MORE.

I'M JUST SPREADING LOVE PICK YA JAW OFF THE FLOOR.

SHARK WITH THE LOANS I BE SWIMMING IN THE DOUGH.

BACKSTROKE I GOT THE BEST FLOAT.

WATCH MY SURFBOARD, HIGH TIDES I'LL WASH IT FOR THE LOW.

PRICE UNPREDICTABLE, I KEEP A BIG GUY OR TWO.

OMG THAT'S FORTY FORTY BAY SEASONING BOO.

IF YOU REALLY A PRINCE I'LL MARRY YOU. ~

CROSS COLOURS JACKETS WHEN I GO TO RE UP.

ONE, TWO, THREE, WE JUST PLAYING RING UP.

SPLIFF MASTER C, I'M GOOD WHEN I D UP.

TEN TOES IN, PLUS MY TWO FEET UP.

A DUB ON THE PACK, ANOTHER ON THE ZADDY SAC.

FURIOUS STYLES, BRING THE BOYS AND THE BEES BACK.

COLORFUL JOURNEYS OF A BUTTAFLY
LYRICS SO PROUD, R-E-S-P-E-C-T THAT.

WHAT THEY WANT NOW?

BECAUSE BUTTA GOT RERACK.

SO BRIGHT, I CAN ONLY BE BLACK.

I'M IN LOVE WITH PARADISE, SWEAR ON GOD, I LOVE MY LIFE.

THEM PLUGS, I SACA TWICE.

GAWEA INDY ICE.

BELIEVE I DO THIS NICE.

WE STARS JUST SHINING BRIGHT.

ALREADY WRITTEN RIGHT?

NO PAUSE JUST FEEL THE BITE.

MY DRAWS THEY VICKI TIGHT. ~

WE GOT THE KEYS, I GOT THE KEYS.

I GO SO HARD PUTTING BS AT EASE.

ROLLING WITH MY SQUAD FROM THE SKY TO THE DIRT.

YUP I GOT MY LIFE BACK BEFORE IT GOT WORSE.

COUPLE SPARES, FEW STRIKES, WHAT DON'T KILL YOU POP FIRST.

PROBABLY WITH AUNTIE TRYING TO GET US A NEW PURSE.

CRENSHAW HIGH LOW BLOWS WON'T HURT.

BACK TO MY SIDE WITH WORD LIKE THE WORK.

I CAN LIVE THIS HERE IN A FUBU SHIRT.

RUNNING MAN, THE WOP, BUTTAFLY OR A TWERK.

HOP OUT ON YA BLOCK JUST PASS ME THE PURP.

HE BE DRIPPING SO GOOD EXCUSE MY SLURP.

CLOSED MOUTH DON'T GET FEED STAR SIXTY-NINE HEAD.

PILLOW PRINCESS SLEEP NUMBER QUEEN BED.

I LEAVE EM WITH THAT, "I WANT WHAT SHE HAD".

TIP THE WAITER, CHECK PLEASE AND A DOGGY BAG.

BLACK GIRL MAGIC SWAG I'M STILL POPPIN TAGS. ~

DAMN CAN A QUEEN BREATH?

I DO LOVE. "ME TOO", NOW ARE YOU FEELING ME?

TRYING TO KICK THESE BLUES, MUDDY WATERS, BB KING.

MESSING WITH THE TUBE BEING ALL I CAN BE.

SALUTE MANY MILES TRAVELED REALLY PAVED THESE STREETS.

COME THROUGH, WE GREW WITH THE FIFTH WARD AND ELM TREES.

BRANCH REACH SO LONG TELL HER BANK PAY ME.

NO MORE TALKING WHEN I WALK UP IN THERE SAFE PLEASE.

FROM THE CABINET TO THE CHAMBERS, I'M SO TRIGGER SAFETY.

OH MY, THERE GOES DANGER, LIFE JACKET SAVE ME.

SO HIGH, WEEZY FLORENCE THEY BOTH MY LADIES.

I NEED MY CHECK, THINGS COME OUT MY MOUTH REALLY CRAZY.

FLOWATREE

COLORFUL JOURNEYS OF A BUTTAFLY
OH WHAT THE HELL, OBAMA PSI PHONE EIGHTY THREE.

BLESS THE GAME AGAIN, I CAN'T QUIT I'M JUST
PLAYING ME.

I DON'T HEAR BEEP BEEP, I KNOW CHOO CHOO AND
SKET SKET.

RAINBOWS AND RAINDROPS, POUR IT UP REE REE. ~

JUST SIGNED A NEW DEAL, MONEY BAGS AND NEW
JEWELRY.

FINNA SMOKED A WHOLE POUND AND YES IT'S
BLUEBERRY.

NOW ALL I NEED IS A GLASS OF SHAY AND
CRANBERRY.

I WAS ON OFF THAT MOLLY TALKING ABOUT MARRY.

I WANT TO TALK TO THE STRENGTH OF SAMSON.

FLY ME TO THE MOON BLUE DREAM HAD ME DANCING.

HEY, CANNABIS, YES I CAN CAN.

PURPLE GRANDAD OIL FOR THE VAPE PEN.

NO YOU CAN'T SMOKE DON'T KNOW WHERE YOUR
HANDS BEEN.

WHITE WIDOW HIGH NOSY NEIGHBOR KEEP THE
GLANCING.

SMOKEY, ON MY PORCH BUT THIS AIN'T NORMANDIE
AND WESTERN.

I NEED ME A BIG PACK NOT A LITTLE TWENTY TWIN
TWIN.

RIDING IN A F-TYPE JAG, TOP BACK HAIR SWINGING.

COME THRU POWER TRAINING, I BE STEAMING.

NEW AGE ASTON MARTIN V12 DREAMING.

MY BOY BLOW IT IN A CARTRIDGE FOR A SEGA AND THE LEANICH.

YOU CAN CARE A VAN THE WHITE JUST DONT TOUCH MY GREENICH.

I BE AROUND DAY AND NITE ALWAYS ON THE SCENE BISH.

MONEY, POWER, RESPECT, I CAN MAKE A KING RICH. ~

I GOT IT I GOT IT FRESH UP OUT THE POT MIX.

TEN TOES UP, I ROCKED OUT LIKE A COCKPIT.

SO OFFICIAL MY WHISTLE MIGHT STOP IT.

MY CREDENTIAL LEAVE A NIGGA WITH OPTIONS.

WHO SAID NOT ME? BUTTA STILL POPPING.

BUST UP IN THIS BISH LIKE, WHAT'S HOPPING.

JUMPMAN, DUMP OFF, ABOUT TO WALK MY STRAPS IN.

HOLD YA BREATH BECAUSE THIS IS AIR MACKING.

SHORE LINES, SEA SHELLS, NO CASES BUT WE PACKING.

BLACK RETAIL ELEVATING ALL TRAPPING.

I DO WELL I MUST SAY IF YOU ASKING.

TOOT MY BELL, MOO SI MOO CAPTAIN.

WHAT THE HELL NIGHT? HANDS STILL CLAPPING.

I MADE A HARD RIGHT.

HAD ME THINKING THAT MY TUNE LEFT.

BUT FROM ME TO YOU, I DO TO DEATH.

THANK GOD I CAN LIVE WITH ALL MY REGRETS.

FLOWATREE

COLORFUL JOURNEYS OF A BUTTAFLY

WHAT DON'T OFF YOU, PUT YOU ON TO NEW SUCCESS.

WE STILL BALANCED, IT'S LESSONS IN THESE STEPS.

PURPLE RAIN, PURPLE HEARTS PUT A METAL ON YA CHEST.

SILVER STARS, S A POPPA AT HIS BEST.

TIMMY TURNED HER ONTO THAT PRINCESS TIANA DRESS.

SO SHE CAN TWIRL LIKE ME NO STRESS.

OVERSEAS COME AND GO AS WE PLEASE, WORLDS BEST.

G.O. GREEN LIGHTERS FLICK IT.

NO TICKETS FORMED AGAINST US, STICKING.

SPENDING CHEESE, YES I'M BIG PIMPIN. ~

SIMPLE AS 1, 2, 3 BUTTATOKOUNMPO.

SPREADING MY WINGS I DON'T SEE WHAT THEY DO.

WHOLEHEARTEDLY I REALLY RESPECT TUNE.

HOES PARDON ME, YES VIDAL SASSOON.

WISHY WASHY STARTED FROM THE BOTTOM ROSE TIPPY TOPPY.

PATIENCE AND VIRTUE NO MORE SLOPPY COPIES.

NEVER GOING TO HURT YOU, IM TRUE AS THE EARTH BLUE.

THANK GOD FOR PUTTING US ON EARTH TOO.

GLORY HALLELUJAH NOW PASS ME THE PURPLE.

LEANING ON MY LORD I BE SIPPING WITH THE BLOOD TOO.

FROM HERSHEY TO HERSCHEL.

LAUGHING REAL LOUD, WE BIG MONEY GOING COMMERCIAL. ~

I'M DEDICATED TO ALL THINGS RELATABLE.

STUCK LIKE KRAZY GLUE.

COUNTING ON MY PAPER MOVES.

SHARPER THAN A SABERTOOTH.

SOUND BITES I ATE A FEW.

THROW BACK A ROUND OR TWO.

I'M TIPSY I CAN ROCK A ROOM.

ON M SKI YES I'M POPPIN TOO.

LORENA I MIGHT CUT A JEWEL.

WHO SENT ME, YOU'LL NEVER KNOW.

WHERE'S THE WEED AT?

ALL THE SMOKE THEY GIVE I BREATHE THAT.

HUFFING AND PUFFING, COOKING UP FEEDBACK.

HUT, HUT, SET. NEVER SET ON REHAB.

I JUST CALL UP THEE NAB.

VIC WITH THE STICK, BIRDIE IF YOU HEARD ME.

QUICK WITH THE LICK, I ALWAYS COME TOO EARLY.

I JUST GOT TO SPIT. THAT'S THE GIRL IN ME.

NO DISRESPECT, I WILL EXCUSE YOUR FEET.

I WALK ON WATER, PART THE SEVEN SEAS.

PICK PURPLE EGGPLANTS FROM THE GARDEN OF EVE.

MAKE IT RAIN DANCE IN SOUTHERN CALIFORN IE

FLOWATREE

    COLORFUL JOURNEYS OF A BUTTAFLY
ME LOVE YOU LONG TIME, THEY SO HORNY.

WE'RE A HAPPY FAMILY, BARNEY.

CORNUCOPIA CHILDREN OF THE CORNY.~

6

BUTTA'S WORTH

For happiness and freedom, I had to step into the flow. I had to place my soul under new management. God does everything according to His purpose. No weapon formed against me nor mine shall prosper, Ashay! God will do it for us. Whatever we make happen for other people, God will do for us. I pronounce benediction over my past. I will laugh more. I will get richer and stronger each day, and I will not let anyone break my peace, Ashay! My crisis is that my Christ is. Thank you, Jesus. My single parent problems, Christ is working on it. My love life issue, Christ is working on it. I trust and believe that God's power is stronger than anyone else's. Our love for the Lord is freeing us from our past, glory be to God! He has been better than good to me. My peace, my unseen, and my safety, Christ is all these things. God works for our good because He is good. Thank you, Lord, for placing me in the hands and arms of a clean king, glory be to God. Thank you for listening, oh Jesus. The word "bless" is "barak" and means "bless God, adored with bended knees". Praise is an outward expression of inward gratitude. Praise is our body's response to our spirit's gratefulness. Our sovereign, the Most High, is an everlasting God, sufficient for our needs. The eternal Creator is our provider, banner, healer, peace, righteous, who is present. The Lord, our Shepherd's mercy, it endureth forever and ever. "Ashay".

FLOWATREE

COLORFUL JOURNEYS OF A BUTTAFLY

WE CAN HELP AND MAKE IT LIGHT ON HIS FEET.

GET RID OF THE DRY SKIN AND SOAK THEM IN SPIRITUALITY.

THEN RUB THEM UNTIL THEY ARE SOFT.

THE FOLKS HE CURE WILL WALK TALL.

GLIDE WITH GRACE.

SMOOTHING OUT ANY CLOTS.

HIS BLOOD FLOWING THRU OUR VEINS WILL NEVER RIOT.

LORD HAVE MERCY ON THE PAIN, SC JOHNSON GANG.

RESTORE OUR STRENGTH, FROM THE WAIST ON DOWN.

SO WE WILL FOREVER DANCE, MARCH, RUN, PLAY, JUMP FOR JOY AND WALK AROUND.

LET'S BE THE BEST STAND UP WE CAN BE, FROM THE CROWN OF OUR HEADS TO THE SOULS OF OUR FEET. ~

I WAKE UP AND THANK GOD MY CAKE UP.

I'M PRETTY AF, ETERNAL MAKE UP.

GET MY MIND RIGHT AND ROLL ROLL MY BAKE UP.

THEN I'M BACK AT IT FEELING LIKE JACOB.

I COOK, CLEAN, AND HUSTLE NO STRUGGLE.

MY SWAGGER GOT BUILD FROM THE MUSCLE.

POPS TOLD ME TAKE CARE OF MY SIBLINGS.

THAT'S WHY I'M ON GO, I GOT TO GET IT.

FIRST LADY I HOLLA BLACK, I HAVE MICHELLE SWAG.

I KEEP THE PEACE AND LOAD THE TRAY IN FIRST CLASS.

BLACK BEAUTY IS SO PRETTY, HELLO BIG MAD.

IF I LET THE HOMIE HIT HE'LL BE A LAB TECH.

EVERY TOM DICK AND HARRY, I CAN'T I CAN'T HAVE THAT.

I'M GOING TO THE BOOK AND IF I LIKE IT I CAN GRAB THAT.

I TOTAL IT ALL UP SO I CAN MAKE MY CASH CASH.

EXPRESS IN THE CLUTCH STACKING PAPER IN MY STASH PAD.

I'M BRINGING CLASS ACT WILDIN ON THAT ASS.

I TRIED TO SCHOOL YOU ON MY LAST MAP AND THEN I FOUND THE GOLD.

REALNESS, I NEVER RAN FROM A TRICK.

LOYALTY IS ALL I KNOW I'LL NEVER MESS WITH A PRICK.

IF I AM IN A PLACE WHERE MY BOTTOM DON'T FIT,

A WHOLE BOTTLE OF MOSCATO THEN I'M LOOKING TO GET RICH. ~

BACK UP IN THIS PEACE LIKE HER SHE GO, AGAIN.

BIG BALLS OUT WATCH MY BACK LIKE BOWLING PINS.

THEY KILLED THE BULL JESUS SAID HE DIED FOR OUR SINS.

IDK I STILL PRAISE HIM BEFORE AND AFTER WINS.

I SEEN THE STRUGGLE REAL LIFE YEA BIG BUNDLES.

FLOWATREE

COLORFUL JOURNEYS OF A BUTTAFLY

DIGGIN ON THE LAST FOR THE TALENT THAT THE PASS DUG YOU.

SUPER SPEED I HIT A FIFTY YARD DASH DOUBLE.

ONE HUNDRED ON THE TRACK YES BUTTAFLY HUSTLE.

I GOTTA KEEP IT TIGHT, I PINKIE PIE TRUST YOU.

UNTIL IT'S ON GLOVES OFF OJ NO JUICE.

I GO TO CHURCH AND YELL BISHOP I GOT YOU.

CLEANING UP THESE PLATES NOW WATCH WHAT THE POTS DO.

I CAME IN THIS WORLD WITH A LOT TO DO.

I AIN'T LEAVING OUT THIS MUTHA LOVER NO TIME SOON.

GIVE MY KIDS A LITTLE SUMPIN SUMPIN TO BRAG ABOUT.

WHEN BUTTA IN THE HOUSE BETTER WAWA WATCH YA MOUTH.

GOT LITTLE BRA AND THEM, TOMMY ON THE FIFTH FLOOR.

HEAD LIKE GINA AND MY MOUTH LIKE PAM COLE.

I GOT MY NAE NAE AND KEYS, BLESS THEIR HALOS.

ON MY MARTIN SHIT, GIRL GO GO.

DRAKE BANGING OUT MY SPEAKERS KEKE I LOVE YOU.

NAE TOO I PUT IT ON MY LIFE I'M GOING TO BUBBLE.

ROCK, PAPER, SHOOT.

NO CHOPSTICKS WON'T DO.

WE AIN'T FIGHTING IN THE STREET LIKE MORTAL DOT COM FOOLS.

I'M THROWING WISH NOT SHADE WE FROM THE SAME STEW.

THROW THEM BAGS BACK I WAS DEDICATED TOO. ~

I DON'T BE WORRIED ABOUT THE NEXT CHICK.

BECAUSE YOU ALWAYS LEAVE ME FEELING LIKE THE BESTEST.

ION LISTEN TO WHAT THE PEOPLE SAY.

THEY DON'T KNOW ABOUT YOU AND ME BABY BAY BAE.

I CAN'T FORGET ABOUT THE TIMES WE SHARED.

THRU THE FOG TO THE SUNNY DAYS OH MY GOD, YOU STILL HERE.

I DONE SHED TEARS, BUST OFF, BUST BACK, SWITCH TRACKS, HELD COMPOSURE OVER COUPLE STACKS.

THANK YOU FOR THE KITES AND DAPS FOR WALL DOE.

FALL THRU ON ANY MAP, CROSSE'S UP AWARD SHOWS.

THAT PRESIDENTIAL BLACK YES LORD KNOWS.

NO MO RUFF DEALINGS,

WE GLOBETROTTING MORE GOALS.

FORGIVE ME FOR ALL THE PUFFIN AND PILL POPPING

OLD FLOWS.

EAST COAST BREED, MY GRIND MODE IS LIKE A WEST OH.

ONLY THE BEST KNOW, COMPRENDE ME CONFESTO.

FLOWATREE

COLORFUL JOURNEYS OF A BUTTAFLY
CONFESSIONS OF A YOUNG BLACK QUEEN FROM
HARRISBURG BRO.

F WHAT YOU HEARD YO, MY BUTTON STAY ON GO.

REBUKING MALARKEY LIKE A PORN STAR.

I KEEP RECEIPTS ON HAND AT MY LAWYERS BAR.

DREAMS OF GETTING RICH IN COMPANY CARS.

PING WITH THE PONG, BET THE BEAT I GO HARD.

SING WITH THE SONG LIKE AN ACOUSTIC GUITAR,
COUGAR OR JAGUAR.

I AM PASS MARS MY ANUS JUST ASK STARS.

NO SHITTING DON'T WANT WAR.

CLOSET SPACE IS FOR AVENTADOR, CRAFTY DON'T
WHORE NO MORE.

ASK EM I NEVER BEEN A BORE.

LIFTED LIKE A CHOIR COURSE HALLELUJAH, LET HIM
DO IT!

I'M THE ONE YOU CAN'T IGNORE, SLICK CHICK BIG
INFLUENCE.

PULL UPS, BIGGER BARS AND BETTER MUSIC.

FOR GIVE ME FOR WHO I AM THE GODS MADE ME DO
IT.~

MY TEARS ARE FOR MY ACCOMPLISHMENT.

I HAD TO LET GO OF THINGS I AIN'T CLICKING WITH.

SO PROUD TO SAY I STUCK WITH IT.

THAT TOWEL SOMETIMES I WANT TO THROW IN.

BUT I USE THAT JOINT JUST TO WIPE ME DOWN.

BOB AND WEAVING FAKE SHOTS I NEED TO SMOKE A POUND.

YEA I WORK THIS LOVE WHEN I HIT THE TOWN.

I KEEP A BELT BUT FOR THE RING, I'LL DO A COUPLE ROUNDS.

I GOT THAT VIA CONNECT GANG AND I KEEP IT WET MAN.

THEY CAN PLAY THEMSELVES BUT CAN'T FOOL MY SET MAN.

I WISH A MOTHER LOVER WOOD FROM FRESH TO DEATH JAMS.

I BOP ON THAT FOOL AND DO A TWO STEP DANCE.

I ROCK, WHIP, SIT AND DIP.

I ROLL MY HIPS LIKE I ROLL MY SPLIFF.

CONTROL THE WHIP, I GHOST RIDE THE LICK.

LUCKING UP BECAUSE I'M HIGH AS WIZ.

I START HIGH AND SHIT.

ROLLING THRU WAVING HI AND SHIT.

YO GET UP GET DOWN WITH THIS.

LAY DOWN FUTURE PLANS UNTIL YOU ARE RICH.

BUILT A CASTLE OUT OF SAND A BRIDGE OVER THE DITCH.

NUMBERS ON THAT BRICK ROAD SO MY KIDS CAN SKIP.

GOLDEN GATES INTERCOM ASKING WHO YOU WIT?

IF YOU GET PASS MY DOGS THEN YOUR COOL TO SIT.

GIVE ME BRAIN, I LET YOU CHAT A BIT.

SO NEVER WASTE THE TABLES TIME.

FLOWATREE

COLORFUL JOURNEYS OF A BUTTAFLY

WE TIME TABLE ALL THE GRIND.

ONE HUNDRED MULTIPLIED BY A POCKET DIME.

COLLECT GANG NOW I'M JINGLING A THOUSAND RHYMES.

I'M THE BEST I POLISH AND I SPIT SHINE.

A GREAT DEBATER WALKING A FINE LINE.

REAL IN THE CATCH, UMPIRE WITH THE SIDE WINDE.

QUICK WITH THE PITCH ALL POSITIONS GAMES MINE.

SAFE, IT'S GOOD. SHE SCORES HOLE IN ONE.

GET YOUR REMATCH UP ON WHO NEXT TO COME. ~

I AM NOT THE BRIGHTEST, I AIN'T FINISH COLLEGE.

HIP WITH THE GRIP BUT I GOT A LITTLE MILEAGE.

SPORTS TEE AND JEANS, I DO LESS STYLING.

TEAM WILD STYLE, WE STAY WILDIN.

PRIVET DANCING ON AN ISLAND.

MIDDLE OF THE KITCHEN PLATES IS PILLING.

FAST FOOD FIGHT, BELLY STILL GROWLING.

BEAST OF THE EAST, BUTTA STAY SMILING.

I'M COLD WITH THE HEAT MOVING FEET THRU THE CROWD MAN.

DON'T SPEAK NOW, KEEP YA TREATMENT ON SILENCE.

CONDUCTING DESTRUCTION I'M NOT WITH THE VIOLENCE.

NAPKIN TUCKED IN, SHOOTER RIGHT BESIDE ME.

"WHO SAID DAT" DON'T YOU TRY IT.

77

JUMP IN A PORSCHE HIT THE ROAD ON SOME HI SIS.

BUTTAFLY DOORS OPEN UP, NOW I'M FLYING.

HIGH SKY BOUND THANKS FOR THE RIDE MAN.

I DO NOW, MORE RINGS LESS CRYING.

I SING PROUD, TWO CHAINZ I'M BUYING.

BIG GIRL LOVE WITH PERFECT TIMING.

SEASONS GREETINGS MARK THE HALL WITH MY INK.

I GIVE YOU TWO KISSES AND ONE WINK.

SWEETER THE JUICE I DON'T LIKE MY MEAT PINK.

RAW DOG MAKE THAT SOUR D STINK.

ALL Y'ALL NEED TO FOLLOW YOU THINK!

THINK OF ALL THE DOPE THINGS YOU BRING.

WE CAN BLOW THIS HERE RIGHT THRU THE ROOF.

WE OWED A GRIP SO F LETTING LOOSE.

I TOLD MY NINJAS I WAS COMING THRU.

KEEP RIDING LADIES, JUMP EVERY BROOM.

SEE MY INTENTIONS IS TO NEVER LOSE.

MY INVENTIONS BRING BETTER NEWS.

I WANT BITCOINS AND LOTS OF JEWS.

FREE GYMS, SCHOOL, HEALTH CARE AND MEDS TOO. ~

I DIDN'T WANT TO VENT BUT I MADE ME.

BACK AT SQUARE ONE, TWO STEP CAN'T FADE ME.

YOU HAD IT GOING ON BUT WHAT TO DO WITH IT?

I HAD TO BOUNCE, I'M NOT GOOD AT PLAYING STUPID.

FLOWATREE

COLORFUL JOURNEYS OF A BUTTAFLY

PUT RESPECT ON MY NAME OR YOU CAN MOVE QUICK.

ALL OF THESE TEST OF TIME AND THESE NEW TITS.

I DIDN'T INVESTING MINE TO GET THE BLUES BISH.

SO DON'T BE NEXT BEHIND THE LOSERS.

I CAN DO GOOD BY MYSELF, I'M USED TO IT.

I NEED THE GOOD LORD TO PICK UP WHERE IT HURT ME.

CARTIER MY WRIST, UMBRELLAS AND NEW PURSES.

LONG WAY DOWN BUT IT WAS WELL WORTH IT.

PICKING UP CRUMBS I DROPPED ON PURPOSE.

ONLY FUMBLE PLAYS THAT MADE ME NERVOUS.

RUG SWEEPING, DUST DAWN TO SURFACE.

PLUG SPEAKING SAID BLOW LIKE CURTIS.

PARTICIPANTS PEAKING, PARTITION CURTAINS.

REPORTING LIVE, LORD HAVE MERCY.

I PROPOSE A HOOK AND A DOPER VERSY.

ACTION CUT, I CHOP BLOCKS AND TURKEYS.

MAXED OUT THEY WONT GET MY PEE.

FROM MY VEST TO THE GATE YOU CAN CHECK NO IDS.

CLASSIFICATION HE JUST A SIDE PIECE.

I MASTERED BATION AT A HIGH DEGREE.

STILL COMING LIKE AN ENGINE INSIDE A V.

TWELVE IS SNELL'S CANT FOLLOW SHE.

FAST AND FEARLESS KEY.

I KNOW THE SPEED AND THE BUSS THAT PASSED ON ME.~

I AIN'T NO FIVE DOLLAR CHICK I'MA BILLION DOLLAR ENTITY.

POWER AND RESPECT, ONLY THOROUGH NINJAS INTEREST ME.

I KNEW IT FROM DAY ONE WE WOULD BE COMPOSED EVENTUALLY.

BUT I AIN'T RUSHING NOTHING BECAUSE HE BLOWS MY MIND MENTALLY.

YEA THE KING IS HOME, I GOT SOME NEW MEAT.

FIRST CLASS A CUTIE.

LIKE A G.T, ME BOO, TWO SEATS AND A KEY.

I'M SMOKING OOH WEE, WHILE HE RUBBING ON ME OOOUUU WE.

THAT'S HOW HE DOES ME, GET ME WET AND THEN SEDUCE ME.

HE RUB MY BOOTY, HA HA GIGGLE MAKE A MOVIE.

MY BOO IS SO HOT DON'T NEED NO FANS, I'M HIS GROUPIE.

YOU CAN'T BELIEVE IT MIND YA BUSINESS, YOU SHOULD DO YOU.

I'M FEELING PRETTY I'M JUST SKATING LIKE NUNU.

BELOVED FOR LIFE, IN A DRESS OR A MUUMUU.

HOLLA HARRISBURG AND I ALWAYS REP MY BOYZ TO.

HEAVY WITH THE CANNON PERFECT WITH THE LANDON.

SEXY WITH THE NECKY GOT ME REACHING FOR MY TECKY.

I AIN'T GOTTA SAY SPIT BUT DO KNOW THEY GOING TO RESPECT ME.

FLOWATREE

COLORFUL JOURNEYS OF A BUTTAFLY
NO HARD FEELINGS I BLESSED YOU, YOU BLESSED ME.

NO WRONG DEALINGS THAT SOFTNESS IS FOR THE
NEXT SEAT.

CUSHION PUSHING TRACKS DAYTONA RIDING HIGH
SPEED.

I'M NEVER GOING BACK TO THE SLOW DRIP AND IV'S.

NOT ME OCKY TO COCKY CAN'T STOP ME.~

MY SKIN SMOOTH LIKE BUTTA AND MY YOU KNOW
THE BEST.
THAT'S WHY I ROCK A S ON MY CHEST.

STEPPING OUT MY COCOON HUNGRY FOR SUCCESS.

EVERY TIME I HIT SNOOZE I THANK GOD WE BLESSED.

WON'T CATCH ME WITH MY HAND OUT LOOKING A
MESS.

IF THEY AIN'T ON YOUR LEVEL DON'T SETTLE FOR
LESS.

IF THEY DON'T BRING IT TO THE TABLE DON'T GIVE EM
NO SEX.

A POWER COUPLE IS WHEN WE BOTH BALLIN CASHING
THEM CHECKS.

SEE THE CHOIR THEY LOVE ME BUT SOME HATERS BE
ILLING.

I DON'T OWE YOU A THOUGHT SO GET THE F OUT YO
FEELINGS.

I'M THE HOTTEST THING GRILLING.

STRONGEST CHAIN DIAMOND CHILLING.

NO MORE RIDDING AROUND GETTING IT.

MY LOVE I'M BACK IN THE BUILDING.

I KILL BEATS I DON'T BEEF.

I GOT TOO MUCH LOVE FOR THE STREETS.

SO IF I RULED THE WORLD, HARRISBURG GOING TO EAT.

I TURN UP I'M A GEEK.

STRAIGHT FACTS WHEN I SPEAK.

I GET MY LOVE FROM THE BOOK I GIVE A F WHAT THEY TWEET.

SEE AT THE END OF THE DAY, IT'S THE BEGINNING OF ME.

DON'T KNOW WHAT THEY HEARD BUT ONE DAY WE'LL SEE.

I'M GONNA KEEP SPITTING ON THESE BARS, BUTTA START WITH A B.

DON'T BE HATING ON SHAE, IT BRINGS THE PAST OUT OF ME.

I CLAP BACK WITH CLASS.

BUTTERFLIES THRU THE STREETS.

MUSTARD SEEDS WITH THE KETCHUP, WHAT A BEAUTIFUL SPRING.

I'M LAYING IN A BED FULL OF ROSES BECAUSE ITS FIT

FOR A QUEEN.

YOU PICKING WEEDS TRYING TO WATER GRASS THAT AIN'T GREEN.

F YOU MEAN~

FLOWATREE

COLORFUL JOURNEYS OF A BUTTAFLY

WHERE THE WHEATIES AT?

ORANGE BOX RACKS IN.

SUGAR SMACKS FOR THE OTHER SIDE BACKHAND.

KEEP YOUR CHIN UP BIG HEAD BLACK MAN.

V.I.C.T.O.R.Y LAP DANCE.

FALL THRU WITH THE GAME MRS. PACK-MAN.

PACK A RAW CONE WITH THE SUPER SACK MAN.

I TAKE IT BACK BECAUSE FAMILY MATTERS.

THIS THE BIG ONE, TOO MY SON AND SANFORD.

WHAT'S UP? CLASSIC TRIP MARTIN CAMPING.

DAMN BRA MAN, CAN YOU MAKE ME A SAMMICH?

THEY NEED TO MANAGE, TO GET THAT STUFF LINED
UP.

WOLF COOKIE, ALWAYS HOWLING FOR BUCKS.

NO NOOKIE COME AGAIN CAN YOU HIT WHAT?

I GOT THE SHOT CLOCK MESSAGE AND THEY TIMES UP.

MY BLESSINGS AIN'T CLICKING WITH NO BAD LUCK.

X CHICKENS TRYING TO RIDE THE WAVE TALKING
ABOUT US.

OLD PICS WONT LET THEM FADE, I HAD TO FLOSS UP.

I NEED THAT HEAD, COIN, TAILS, TOSS UP.

MAILBOX FULL OF DOUBLE MG'Z BOSS UP.

VL DREAMS OF ME CRUISING IN A BENZ TRUCK.

MY FRIENDS AND THEN SOME, BIG WHEELS RED RUM.

A TOAST FOR THE HUSTLERS, HUSTLERS I AM ONE.

FROM EAR DRUMS TO KINGDOM COME.

SO DIPLOMATIC AND I HAVE YET TO RUN.

I JUST FOLLOW THE PATTERNS AND THEN MY
BLESSINGS COME. ~

I RUN THROUGH GREENWOOD WITH BERNICE.

FROM ROWLAND TO DUNKING D'S.

RICH SOCCER MOM IN A YUP THAT'S ME.

YES HOT COLD COMMODITY.

I MASTERED MY SHIT AIN'T NO OUTING ME.

I GOT POWER ON POWER, YOUNG KINGS AND QUEENS.

I GET KNOWLEDGE BY THE HOUR THAT STACKS AND
DREAMS.

I CAN MAKE IT SHOWER I RATHER SEE THE SUN BEAM.

I CAN GROW A FLOWER THROUGH THE BRICK
CONCRETE.

I'M SO WITH THE SHIT SO PLEASE DO SNEEZE.

FLOW JOE WITH THE SPRINT PUSH START AND KEYS.

BUTTAFLY KUSH AND I TOKE ON THE D.

I PROMOTE TEAM WE, BEING ALL I CAN BE.

I CAN VOTE YES I'M FREE.

IF I DON'T STILL KOOL BEANS.

VOLTS LIKE THAT WAGON ON ME.

MS. PARKER, A ACE P.

MISS BERRY BLACK JUICE SWEET.

I'M WITH THE GRADE A- TEAM.

FLIPPING CHIPS FOR THE GREEN. ~

FLOWATREE

COLORFUL JOURNEYS OF A BUTTAFLY

SHAW UNIVERSITY TO OKC,

ALL MY SICILY TYSONS CAN ROCK THE BEAT.

MOTHER NATURE YES LORD WE BIRTH KINGS.

THIS IS MORE THAN REAL HOW WE MOVE THEM THINGS.

STEADY WORKING HARD FOR THE JOY HE BRINGS.

ANY PRESSURE, TEARS AND BLOOD JUST BOOST THE QUEENS

WE DON'T CRUMBLE BLACK BEAUTY LIVES.

CHECKING OUT LATE AND BORN WITH FIRST DIBS.

HUSTLE HARD AND CELEBRATE, WE DO IT FOR THE KIDS.

EXPANDING PROSPERITY WITH ALL THAT WE GIVE.

COOKIES AND BOGEYS NONE OF OUR SOLDIERS ARE FOLDING.

WRIST READY TO ROLLY MY PROTECT LIKE A GOALIE.

WHERE IS MY MILLI DON'T HOLD ME I KNOW MY WORTH.

I WANT MORE THAN YOU OWE ME GOD BLESS MOTHER EARTH.

7

NO CLICHE'

What does equality mean to you? Thank God we are free at last; freedom will last. The power to do what you want to do. The state of not being a slave. The ability for folks to move and act freely. How can we keep these happy feelings in the air? We are children of God celebrating the "Emancipation of African Descendants". It took two and a half years after Lincoln's, University Skills, issued "the Emancipation Proclamation" on June nineteenth in Galveston, Texas, announcing again, the free slaves are set free. We now have a federal holiday on June nineteenth of every year, acknowledging the end of slavery. Commemorating African American culture, education, forms of reparations, massive liberation, economic freedom, Black history, equality, and inclusion. Mercy, grace, and strength for all those standing together to reject all forms of racism. The Lord has made this a day full of festivals, cookouts, concerts, and parties to engage, empower, reach, and teach as we continue the fight for justice. Black folks have been creating system-wide resources for years. In the year of 1863, it was established that all enslaved "shall be then, hence forward and forever free". Jubilee Day is full of melanin power, bringing truth to the nation's people of color. The high energy source on this day helped to create black entertainment like Essence festivals, car shows, food, fun, music, and families. The state of Black America must become a place of positive vibes for all God's people. Holy God, break every chain of trauma off of us in the mighty name of Jesus.

EVIL REPUBLICANS SHALL REAP WHAT THEY SOW.

POSITIVE POLITICIANS WILL BOUNTIFULLY GROW.

CHILDREN OF ALL COLORS WILL SAFELY COME AND GO.

GOD WILL BLESS OUR LAND WE ALREADY KNOW.

MORE KINGS AND QUEENS OF ANOINTED LEADERSHIP.

BLESSED BE THE LORD WHO DAILY LOADETH US WITH BENEFITS. ~

CORETTA SCOTT KING, MARRIED A COURAGEOUS MAN, WHO FOUGHT FOR EQUAL RIGHTS THROUGHOUT THE LAND.

WHEN CLAUDETTE COLVIN SAT IN THE FRONT OF THE BUSS, SHE BEGAN THE FIGHT OF FREEDOM FOR US.

THE BOYCOTT OF PUBLIC BUSSES AND TRANSPORTATION WAS TO PROTECT THE CITY WIDE SPREAD OF RACIAL DISCRIMINATION.

THE NON VIOLENCE THAT JOHN LEWIS CARRIED THROUGH THE JIM CROW SOUTH, WAS A MANTLE OF MORAL AUTHORITY FOR BLACKS IN THE WHITE HOUSE.

THE NATIONAL ASSOCIATION OF COLORED WOMEN MOTTO, IS "LIFTING AS WE CLIMB" IN WHICH TODAY WE STILL FOLLOW. ~

RECONSTRUCTING BIZ PREPARING FOR THE FACE OFF.

THE SQUARE ROOT OF SOUR DIESEL THEN I BREAK OFF.

IT'S THREE SIDES TO EVERY STORY SO I PLAY SOFT.

HARD BALL FOR THE WIN WHEN I PLAY BALL.

I BALL OUT A LITTLE BIT ON MY DAYS OFF.

NO DAYS OFF TRACK I AM RAILROADING WITH TRACK STARS.

LITTLE HEMI THINK I COULDN'T BUT I DID DOG.

I REV UP YOUR REVEREND MAS JIG SAWS.

TICK TOCK, SKIP ROCKS HOPSCOTCH WATCH.

LORD OF MERCY I WANT EVERYTHING I DON'T GOT.

I'MA GET IT WITH A PLAN AND A BIGGER PLOT.

I GO FROM TANNING IN THE SAND TOO A WITCH DOC.

BUTTA PECAN, JUNGLE FEVER AND THEM CHICKEN STOCKS.

GETTING HEAD BUT I CAN TELL WHO'S CHICK IS GIVING TOP.

DJ CAN CUT THE BEAT I STILL WON'T STOP.

UNTIL THEY OPEN UP AND TEAR DOWN THEM CELL BLOCKS.

I'M RIDING FOR ALL MY NINJAS WATCH.

EVEN FUCK CRACKERS KNOW REAL WOMAN RUN THE BLOCK.

YEA I SAID FUCK A CRACKER, NIGGA WHAT.

AND I WON'T TAKE IT BACK, I'M SO UP FRONT. ~

FLOWATREE

COLORFUL JOURNEYS OF A BUTTAFLY

NEW B DAY WISHES, ZODIAC PIMPING.

CLOCKED OUT PROPER, O.E. SIPPING.

IT'S ME HOE, UNSALTED BUTTER DRIPPING.

KING CRAB LEGS IS THE ONLY THING WE DIPPING.

TOAST TO THE GOOD LIFE, YEA I'M A HOOD WIFE.

DON'T NEED TO SUCK OR SLURP ON FIRST SIGHT.

MIGHT POP OR TWERK, IF YA GAME TIGHT.

JUMP LIKE MIKE, MY BAD A LITTLE RUFF RUFF.

I JUST OVER RIDE IT, SO GLAD I DON'T CUFF CUFF.

TWO DOWN FAM TIP ONE, TWO, UP UP.

BIG BALLS SOFT HITS, I BUNT BUNT.

I CAN GET, GET WHAT YOU WHAT.

I'M GREAT, WITH THE FRONT.

NO LACE, LOOK NO HANDS, STRINGS NO TRACE.

SO STOP WORRYING AND JUST FIX YO FACE.

I BEEN DROPPED AND WASHED AT THE CHILDREN'S PLACE.

THE SPA, THAT'S A DATE.

FROM THE FIRST TO THE THIRD NO WAIT.

FIT IT IN, DON'T RUN HER UP, NEVER LAST PLACE.

COME THRU WITH REAL RULES OR I WILL WAIT.

I NEED REAL JEWELS ANNA MAE CARROT CAKES.

NASA'S FINEST AT A MASTERS DEBATE.

I WANT A CLASSIC ESTATE.

MY DAUGHTERS LAMBORGHINI SKATES, PRIVATE ISLANDS AND LAKES.

I AIN'T GOT NO TIME FOR THE HATE.

STILL COUNTING MONEY THAT'S TEN YEARS AGED.

TEN TIMES TEN FOR THE FORTUNE WHEN I FLIP AN OLD PAGE. ~

I'M THE GHETTO GODDAUGHTER, LET'S GET RIGHT.

YOUNG STAY TUNED INTO WHAT IT REALLY LOOK LIKE.

DON'T DRINK SPARKLING WATER AND I STEEL KEEP IT THIGH.

I AIN'T NEVER QUITTING, I'M GOING IN AND UP WITHOUT A FIGHT.

REMY GIRLS I GOT MY TRACKS SEWED UP.

SKATING ON THE ICE WITH THE BEARS SLAM THE PUCK.

WATCH WHAT YOU DOING GOD DAMN WHAT THE WHAT.

STEP ON MY FEET AND MY HANDS GO UP.

GOD BLESS YA SOUL SINCE YOU THINK YOU SO TUFF.

I DUST OFF MY SISTAS WE DIAMONDS IN THE RUFF.

I DON'T MIND PASSING OFF, I PUFF PUFF.

ON MY FRENCH VANILLA BROWN MONTANA HEAR ME NOW.

I PUT IT DOWN WHEN I WANT, I'M A BOSS WITH MY ROUNDS.

ROSS WITH THE GROWL FLY FLOSS AND A SMILE.

MADE IT THROUGH THE PAIN CAN'T NOTHING STOP US NOW. ~

COLORFUL JOURNEYS OF A BUTTAFLY

IF I PASS THE BALL I STILL GOT IT ALL.

I BE PITCHING, FISHING, TENNIS, SOCCER, LAPS MY DOG.

CREATING SOCIAL CHANGE, I CAN WALK THE TALK.

BLESSED BE THY NAME SO I KEEP THE SPARK.

WORKING ON MY NEXT BOOK, "OVERFLOW".

YEAH I SAID IT FIRST, PATENTING MY DOUGH.

THE MORE I SMOKE THE BIGGER THE PHILLY GETS.

I BE RIDING BIG WILLIE ON ALL TYPES OF TIPS.

I MACK BOOK A WISH THEN FLIP THE SCRIPT.

YOUR DOING JUST FINE THAT BS, FORGET.

WE LIT. OUR VICE PRESIDENT IS BLACK.

MY MAYOR IS TOO AND I BE GODDAMN IF WE EVER GOING TO LOSE.

MOLASSES BLACK BERRY I'M SWEETWATER JUICE.

THIRST TRAP SHAWTY THEY BE COMING THRU.

SIS BE WITH THE BOOSTING I HAD TO COP THE TOOLS.

ROCKET LIKE I'M HOUSTON, FIFTH WARD WEEBIE.

I CAN MAKE IT BOUNCE BY MYSELF TO THE B BEAT.

EDGES ON FLE FLEEK, BUNDLES ON DIZ ECK.

B. HOLIDAY I GOT THAT DOPE GIRL SWAG.

THAT DOPE GIRL BAG MAKES THEM NOPE BOYS MAD.~

THEM CHECK INS TO CHECK OUTS.

I'M FEELING IT, I'M FEELING GOOD SO I STICK AROUND.

WHAT'S REALLY GOOD ON THIS SIDE OF TOWN.

I STAY UP DON'T NEED TO KNOW WHATS GOING DOWN.

I'M JUST HERE FOR THE REAL AND THE TIME WE CAN BE.

DON'T KNOW ABOUT YOU BUT I KNOW WHO SENT ME.

ONE TOO MANY I GET CONFUSED WITH FRIENDLY.

DON'T NEED A BENSON I WANT A BENTLEY.

DON'T WANT THEY TWO CENTS, I WANT A TEN SPEED.

RIDE IT HOW I WANT, MIGHT POP UP AND DO A WILLIE.

FOR THE WORLD CRAIG NOT JENNY'S.

MOUTH PIECE CHEW IT UP I GOT PLENTY.

DJ SCREW, OJ AND HENNEY.

BLESSED GIFTED BLACK THIRTY-TWO INCH REMY.

I'M JUST MINING MY BUSINESS, COLE WORLD.

GETTING RICH WITH MY SISTAS, YES GO GIRL.

STUNTING IS A HABIT GET LIKE ME.

HAVE YOU EVER SEEN A CHEVY WITH THE BUTTAFLY SEATS?

JUST TRYING TO BUILD IN GOD'S WORLD WHERE WE ALL THINK FREE. ~

FLOWATREE

COLORFUL JOURNEYS OF A BUTTAFLY

WRITE LIKE A BUTTAFLY BUILD FROM A G.

A LITTLE POCAHONTAS BLOOD A LOT OF PERSONALITY.

I BEEN A CLEAN UP WOMAN SINCE THE AGE OF SIXTEEN.

DID DIRT WITH REAL NIGGAS AND WE STILL SQUEAKY CLEAN.

EYES ALWAYS BE ON CHINK.

I BOUNCE BACK OFF DA PINK.

TIME TO FAST.

COUNT MY BLESSINGS, TWERK AND BANG A LOT OF BEATS.

PERSONAL ROLLER COASTER AND RIGHT NOW I'M AT MY PEAK.

SNEAKY NIGGAS DISTANT SISTAS GOT ME ONLY TRUSTING ME.

I SAY SELF? SELF SAY YES? DON'T GET LONELY AND DEPRESSED.

A GREAT FORCE FROM WITHIN GET THIS STRESS UP OFF MY CHEST.

NEVER BEEN A BIG SPEAKER I RATHER LYRICALLY EXPRESS.

SELF CONSCIOUS ABOUT MY BODY BUT MY BARS BE THE BEST.

FOUND MY MAJOR KEYS AND I WEAR THEM AROUND MY NECK.

LIKE LATIFAH I AM A QUEEN I LOVE MUSIC AND MY SET.

YEA I GET A LOT OF THINGS BUT GETTING LOVE FEELS

THE BEST.

ALL ABOUT THE FREEDOM, PEACE AND HAPPINESS. ~

ITS BUTTA WHEN I SLIDE THRU.

I DON'T CARE WHO ION WHO.

I KEEP THAT ON MY SIDE TOO.

D UP I DRIVE DA ROZAN.

PUSH START, I KNOW HE LOVES ME.

I ROAD IT UNTIL HIS TOES BEND.

IT'S HARD TO QUIT WHAT I LOVE TO DO.

CLIMB HIGHER, DIG WIDER, FLICK A BIC AND UP YOUR LIGHTERS TOO.

NIGHTINGALES TO THEM REVERSE MISTY BLUES.

SO MUCH TIME JUST TO REHEARSE AND KILL THE STEW.

EAT UP SUGAR, I'MMA KEEP SERVING YOU.

IF YOU CRY, CRY FROM THE LOVE OVERDUE.

WHO I?

I BE THAT, ALL OVER YOU.

POWER LIKE GHOST, SO I CALL YOU BOO.

COACH SAID GET EM, I'MA GET EM.

85 SOUTH THANKING GOD IN A RENTAL.

STILL THE FIRST LADY, MRS. ALWAYS PRESIDENTIAL.

THE LIFE THAT I'VE BEEN THRU, I WRITE IT SO SIMPLE.

WALKING IN MY YEEZY BOOTS, WORK IT LIKE KIM DO.

THANK YOU, THANK YOU, THANK YOU, TO MY EX'S

FLOWATREE

COLORFUL JOURNEYS OF A BUTTAFLY

AND HER TOO.

RUNWAYS TO RUN JOES, TIPPING ON MY TOES.

OH MY D.O. DOUBLE GIZZLE ONLY GOD KNOWS.

FEW PODS AND BLOGS, THIS IS MY EYE SHOW.

HE LIKES IT WHEN I TAKE IT OFF, RED LIGHT SPECIAL.

SNEEZING ON THE TRACK I HAD TO SAY BLESS YOU.

HE MAKES A GOOD POINT AND YOU KNOW ABOUT THE REST BOO. ~

I FOUND FIFTY FIVE THO IN THE STASH, NO MORE GREEN MILE LIST.

I GOT TWENTY FIVE QUEENS WITH THE BLICKY THAT WILL BLING BLOWE RICH.

I BRING BLM TO TRIAL I GOT THAT COCHRAN GRIP.

IF THE GLOVE DON'T FIT THEN I QUIT.

IF YOUR PLUG NEVER SNITCHED SHE'S A GIFT.

I KEEP MY KEYS NOW WATCH BUTTA WHIP.

I DON'T AIM TO PLEASE, I'M FLIPPING BIG CHIPS.

I AIN'T NO ACTRESS.

I'M ON THE SIDE WITH LIGHTS, CAMERA, ACTION.

I GOT FREEDOM FOR SALE, WHO WANTS TO BUY A BIT?

COINS AND WISHING WELLS, A CRYPTO SCIENTISTS.

HORNS AND BIG OL BELLS, SO DON'T YOU TRY TO DISS.

IF YOU THOUGHT I FAIL, I'M SUPPLYING IT!

RHYMES AND EQUITY, SIMPLIFYING COMPLEXITY.

TRADING WITH SOME TECH'S AND GEEKS, GROWING

MILLION DOLLAR SEEDS.

I JUST WANT TO MAKE MY MOMS AND POPS PROUD OF ME.

I JUST GOTTA A TOUCH A BILLION BEFORE I LEAVE.

8

TOUCHE' STADIUM

"I be pitching, fishing, tennis, soccer, laps with my dog." Okay team, we must learn the rules to the game, to provide tools and opportunities to impact others. We are creating greater access for people of color in sports. Continuing to raise awareness about giving toward black organizations is changing sports and opportunities. I started by studying black sports analytics, creating a journey to how the advent of pushing the ball brings big data, sports science, marketing, tickets, individual performance, and entrepreneurship. Make winning an attitude and let your defense be your offense. Own the game, don't play yourself. Support ideas and projects to get more black coaches on the field and on the courts. Nelson Mandela once said, "All forms of physical activity that contribute to physical fitness, mental well-being, and social interactions are the tolerance of promoting sustainable development; it is empowering women and contributing to social inclusion." Executive leaderships in sport analytics create pathways to lasting black prosperity. We will not ignore the physical and emotional rights of our people. We will encourage sports economic development of the inner cities athletic programs and business. I've witnessed an AI in the sports world who put forward that, "There's a lot of power, and a lot of wealth as black athletes. Bridging tech and sports, protecting assets, and investing in tech stocks. All these things create ownership and collective bargaining for us to have a piece of the pie" a quote from warrior Andre Iguodala. Another famous AI once said, "I don't wanna be Jordan, I don't wanna be Bird or Isaiah, I don't wanna be any of those guys. I want to look in the mirror and say I did it my way," says the great Allen Iverson. We were built for expansion family, so expand your team capacity and together we will win. Amen.

I ROCK THE VOTE, THEN I TWERK A LITTLE.

I'M THE SHIT IN THE BACK, YUP I WORK THE MIDDLE.

SKEET TO MY DEW, I TIP ROCK AND RIDDLE.

IS MY ROCK IN HERE OR MY TIM'S TOO LITTLE?

Y'ALL GOING TO LET ME ON THIS BIKE WATCH ME PEDDLE!

PUT A HUGGIE IN MY RIM SO YOU CAN HEAR ME BETTER.

PUT YA LADY ON, HOPE SHE CAN HANDLE BARS.

STRETCH WRATH IN MY DREAMS I CAN SEE THE STARS.

SUPER BOWL GOALS, SMASH MOUTH HITS, TOUCHDOWN FLOWS.

WNBA DREAMS, COULD OF BETTER SHO DID SHOW.

BRUCE LEE ROY WITH THE SKILLS KICKING DOWN DOORS.

I'MA GIVE YOU A LIL BIT, PAY ATTENTION MORE.

WATCH THE RIGHT MAN, LEFT HAND GOT BIGGER SHIT IN STORE.

FLOWATREE

COLORFUL JOURNEYS OF A BUTTAFLY
AMBIDEXTROUS, SEXINESS BUT LESS WHORE.

MESSAGE! GET, GET, GET MORE.

EURO STEPPING O.V.O VER, WORLD TOURS.

DATS IT KEEP STEEPING F THEY FLOOR.

THAT'S THE SOUND OF THE BLACK MAN WORKING ON A
NEW PLAN.

SAME UNCLE SAM BUT THE SNAKES DO CHANGE. ~

I LOVE TO DO WHAT'S IN MY HEART.

REAL REP REAL FEEL THE SPARK.

TEN TIMES TEN MAKE MY MARK.

I RUN IT BACK LIKE TAUSHAE SHARPE.

PICK IT BACK UP WE THE BEST.

STARTUPS, SHINE SO BRIGHT.

ANY DAY ALL BLUNT.

I'M GOOD WITH THE STEEL, SUNDAY PUNTS.

SISTER MARY CLEARANCE IN A ST LAURENT.

I GOT THAT ACT RIGHT WHAT YOU WANT?

SPEEDING ON THE FREEWAY.

TWO STEPS BACK I'MA TAKE THE LEAD WAY.

PINKY RING ON ICED OUT WE DAY.

SELF CENTERED, MIDDLE FINGERS TO IN THEE WAY.

STILL OFF MY BACK D WADE.

REAL NIGGA SHIT, YES A UNION OF TRUST.

SEND YOU ON YOUR MERRY WAY IF YOU AIN'T
PRAYING WITH US.

I BE ON THAT MARY J WHEN I'M PUFFIN AND STUFF.

I'M JUST LIVING FOR THE DAY I HAVE MILLIONS OF BUCKS.~

PLEASE DON'T BE FOOLED BY THE PRETTY FACE.

FRONTING WHEN I KNOW THE OLD YOU THIS IS MYSPACE.

BARS ON DECK WILL HAVE YOU MOVING IN YOUR PLACE.

I CAN NEVER LOSE I WILL ALWAYS BE SUPER GREAT.

I'M SERVING UP LAST SUPPER, I'M AMAZING GRACE.

THE FOOD FOR THOUGHT I GOT COULD LEAVE THEM WITH A BETTER TASTE.

I SPIT HOT FIRE ON SOME DYLON SHIT.

I SWEAR TO GOD I CAN'T STOP I GOT THE I-IRON FIST.

FLOAT LIKE A BUTTERFLY I'M STINGING LIKE A SCORPION.

CHOP YOU UP LIKE SUEY TANK YOU HONEY COME AGAIN.

UNLESS YOU AIN'T FROM ROUND HERE, THEN

WHO LET YOU IN?

SEVERE WEATHER WARNING, I AM THE WIN.

AFTERMATH WE BE CALLING UP YOUR NEXT TO KIN.

I'M SQUAD UP AND I WILL TAG THEM IN.

BE GLAD TO SHOW ALL THE TRASH THE BAGS AGAIN.

KISSES IN THE WIND, FACE TOOK IT ON THE CHIN.

YEA THEY TRIED IT GOOD GAME GOOD SPORT.

FLOWATREE

COLORFUL JOURNEYS OF A BUTTAFLY

I DON'T JUDGE I JUST RULE THIS IS MY COURT.

I STAY AHEAD OF THE STRESS LIKE A LONG RESORT.

A WARRIOR I BLESS THE KING LIKE A NEWPORT.

THE CHAMP IS HERE!

YOU NEW TO THIS? I'M TRUE TO THIS!

GOING HAM THIS YEAR IF SKINNY BLACK I'M LUDA CHRIS.

LITTLE, LITTLE CUPCAKE IS JUST A ROOKIE.

I HUSTLE AND FLOW LIKE THE OLD COOKIE.

AND GOD IS GREATER THAN MY HATERS SO DON'T PUSH ME.

ALL THEM CATS YOU RUN WITH, THEY ALL PUSSY.

ALL STATE STAND, YOUR IN GOOD HANDS.

PISTOLVANIA LEAVE YOU BLESSED IN YOUR OWN LAND.

TAT TAT WHAT THE FUCK YEA WE THAT WAY.

I SEEN A LOT OF SORE LOSERS FROM THAT GUN PLAY.

SO I ONLY COME TO SPIT.

I LET MY GOONS SPRAY.

A CELEBRATION FOR THE QUEENS, HAPPY BIRTH WAY.

~

SHAE BUTTA BOOGIE.

I'M TB IN A HOODIE.

FLYING ALL TIME HIGH, YOU GOOD I'M GOODY.

I GOT THAT DRIP C-FIVE TIMES TWO.

RUB IT IN, RUB IT DOWN, COCK, BUST, THEN SHOOT.

BLOW A POUND, COMING HEAVY IN MY WAY YES MOVE.

BUT IF YA CHICK THICK I WANT TO SEE HER WIN TOO.

TYCOON WE CAN GO TRICK FOR TRICK IN THE FUN ROOM.

NEED TO SEE IF YOU CAN MAKE IT TO THE END ZONE.

RBI, HOLE IN ONE OR A FLIP PHONE.

AT THE GUTTA BOWL AND I'M STRIKING OFF THAT SUPERDOME, MARICON'.

NOPE! THIS AIN'T FIESTA FIESTA!

THIS IS BIG MOMMA'S HOUSE AFTER CHURCH STILL DRESSED UP.

AT THE TABLE PLAYING SPADES LIKE ITS YOUR CUT.

THE DEALER RULES, SIDE BETS, GET YOUR CASH UP.

FLIP IT, ABOUT TO TUNK OUT BEFORE YOU DROP.

ALL THAT MONEY PILING UP ALWAYS GET THE POT.

SMOKING ON THAT STRONG LOVE AND I CAN'T STOP.

HOLDING ON WITH ONE GLOVE, KING OF POP TO MOON ROCKS.

SAFETY NO SLUGS, MY BELLS WILL GIVE THE DRUMMER SOME.

EIGHT O EIGHT AND MORE PLUGS, IT ELECTING US.

IT'S ELECTRIC, THEY DON'T WANT THIS THUNDER DUMB.

OH MY GOD OH MY GOD ONE AND ONE.

FRONT LINE FOR THE FIGHT WHO THE TYPE TO RUN?

FLOWATREE

COLORFUL JOURNEYS OF A BUTTAFLY

FINISH LINE WITH THE W BEFORE THE GUN.

READY SET GO HARDER.

I'M A MOTHER, LOVER, SISTER, DAUGHTER.

HOLDING UP THE WALL VP AT ALL THE PARTIES.

NOW WE SEE THE CLOUT, CONTROL THE INS AND OUTS.

THANK GOD BLACK FIST UP IN THE WHITE HOUSE, WRECK IT LIKE RALPH.

LIBERTY AND JUSTICE, FOR JUST US.

WE AIN'T TAKING NO MORE CUTS.

FAIR ACTS, NEW LAWS, A UNION OF TRUST.

MORE WOMEN IN OFFICE, COLORFUL BOSSES.

DON'T TAKE MUCH FOR OUR FUTURE TO COST US.

GOT TO GROW UP, SAY NO TO WAR SHIT.

PLANT THE RIGHT SEEDS, LORD FORGIVE MY ABORTIONS.

KEEP A TIGHT SQUEEZE LETTING OFF GODLY EXTORTION'S.

YEA I MIGHT BE, DON'T JUDGE US, NOT IN YOUR COURT SEAT.

UNLESS MY GIRLS ARE DUNKING ON YOUR TEAM. ~

AIN'T NOTHING TO A QUEEN LIKE ME.

I TAKE A DOPE MASTER BEAT AND TURN IT TO A

MASTERPIECE.

WHERE I'M FROM I DON'T WANT TO C MURDER, SHOUT OUT TOO MASTER P.

BLESSED TO LIVE THRU IT ALL TO SAY I'M LIVING LIKE

A G.

GO NO LIMIT, BE ALL YOU CAN BE.

YOU GOTTA LOVE AND LEARN TO FIND YOURSELF, F WHO DON'T SEE.

I KEEP MY EYE ON THE PRIZE AND HE IS BIGGER THAN THE SEA.

I CAN SWIM WITH ANY SCHOOL THE BIGGEST FISH THAT BE ME.

MIGHT SLIP, NEVER AN L, LIKE SEAN I BOUNCE BACK.

I'M IN HAIR LIKE REMY YUP ONE HUNDRED ON THE TRACK.

I AM STAR WITH THE GAME YOU CAN CALL ME MRS. DAK.

IF I BUY A BAG OF DIRT BET MY NINJAS RUN IT BACK.

SWIFT LIKE EMMITT SMITH RUSHING RECORDS IS MY GIFT.

I GOT THE GIFT OF GAB YOU BLINK AND I MIGHT MAKE A WISH.

I MIGHT TAKE FOUR CUT AND MAKE SIX.

FEELING LIKE A WICKED WITCH WALKING ON THESE BRICKS.

BUT THIS IS KANSAS YO, I GOT GAS IN MY CANS THOUGH.

I AIN'T LYING WANNA SEE I LET YA MANS BLOW.

STINGY WITH MY COOKIES SO KEEP IT IN YA PANTS BRO.

YEA HE TRIED ME BUT I DABBED AND HIT EM WITH THE WHOA. ~

FLOWATREE

COLORFUL JOURNEYS OF A BUTTAFLY

MBJ TOO MJ DON'T LET THE FLEX FOOL YOU.

BIG BRON HAIR TRIGGER, T-REX RUGGER.

MOVIE MAKER, WE GET THE PAPER.

AS-SALAMU LAKE EM WITH THE LAKERS.

BISH ME LA TO THE CAVS.

STEADY PACING LIKE A PACER.

DO MY THING LIKE A MAV.

I NEED A RICK FOR THE RAKE UP.

I GOT A RAPTOR. A RAPTURE OF ROCKETS.

BRING THE NETS OUT, TELL THE BULLS TO BLOCK IT.

F IT BUCKETS, HEAT THE NUGGETS.

SLOW BRICKS, BUTTA CHURNING KINGS AND KNICKS.

SPUR SPLURGING WITH THE PICS.

ER BEFORE THE SIX.

"CLASS OF 03" STOLE THE CHIP.

COUGARS WHO YOU WIT?

I KNUCK FOR THE BUCKS

OKC I GOT THAT MAGIC, GOOD LUCK ~

I CAN ROCKET BABY LIKE CAPELA,

STANDING PROUD I'M THE HIGHEST ON MY LEVEL.

KNOCKING DOWN BARRIERS AND BUILDING UP THE GHETTO.

GROWING STRONG WITH THE CARRIERS, MELODIES AND MEADOWS.

GOOD GIRLS AND THE FELLAS.

EVERYDAY STAY AT YA BEST, SO TOMORROW WON'T GET JEALOUS.

IN THE WAY OF OUR SUCCESS IF THEY MAD THEY SHOULD TELL US.

PSYCH KEEP IT TO YOURSELF RAIN DANCING NO UMBRELLAS.

HELL YEA HEAVEN KNOWS, WHO'S UP TO NO GOOD AND WHO IS DOWN TO ROLL.

ARE YOU REALLY ABOUT THIS LIFE?

WILL YOU FAKE OR FOLD?

WHEN MY ARMS EXTEND, I GOT THE GRIP OF GOLD.

KEEP A BAG OF TRICKS, I CAN LET YOU HOLD.

HAD TO FLIP MY M'S, YES I'M RICH IN SOUL.

SOUL FOR REAL RAP TOO MY CANDY TOES.

WALK ONE WAY, YES LORD KNOWS.

START MY DAY OFF WITH A CUP OF RAINBOWS. ~

YOU CAN TESTIFY "WE THE BEST" THAT RIDE.

THOTS FLOATS THE WAVE, I GIVE YOU JET SON RISE.

BENCH PRESSING SPIRITS, THE CHAIR SIT OR HEAR IT.

THEM PEP RALLIES TOO ALLEYS.

I BRING THEM OUT THEN CLEAR IT.

BRAVE HEART ON THE LIST. J HARDEN I ASSIST.

NO SORRY JUST PARTIES FOR OUR TARDINESS.

I NEVER WORRY I GOT LIGHT IN A DARK ABYSS.

FLOWATREE

COLORFUL JOURNEYS OF A BUTTAFLY

I GLOW LIKE JORDAN WITH THE JUMP SPARKLE SIS.

FLOW LIKE FLORIDA WITH THE PUMP, FEMA CHICK.

OH MY GLORY GIVE IT TO HIM THANKS FOR THE GIFT.

NO I WON'T STOP TELLING STORIES UNTIL WE SUPER RICH.

I ROCK THE BELLS IN THE LAND WHERE WE TWO LEGIT.

I CAN TELL AND SMELL YA LINES AIN'T GARBAGE KID.

WE MINE AS WELL MAKE THEY NOISE ASS OUR AUDIENCE.

IN A MANOR CONFORMING WITH ACCORDANCE.

SUPREME TEAM GOTA MAINSTREAM.

SPREAD LIKE BUTTA CREAM.

GANG GANG JUSTICE FOR JUST US.

BLAME GAME BUT WHO GOING TO STEP UP? ~

FROM THAT JAGGED EDGE ALL THE WAY TWO CHAINZ.

MY GOOD LUCK CHARM YES LORD STILL BLINGS.

BIG CHEESE INDEFINITELY TO BLAME.

BIG RINGS COLLECTIVELY WE CLAIM.

I CAME I SAW I CAME AGAIN TO BALL.

BACK TO PLAQUES THE WALL, NEW FAME OF HALL.

ONE TWITCH AND A SPARK I'M LIKE ARSONAL.

IF WE KISS IN THE DARK THEN IT'S LOVE GALORE.

I'M PEEPING MORE, YOU KEEPING SCORE? WINNING CIRCLE.

YOU SEE THAT DOOR JUST COME OR GO WITH A PURPOSE.

MIND OVER MANNERS, SERMONS ALWAYS AT YOUR SERVICE.

SO GIVE FOR THE LOVE AND FORGIVE ALL THAT UNDONE.

IF YOU WOULDN'T DID WHAT YOU DID, I STILL BE NUMB.

SPENT TIME WITH THE KID AND YOU LEARNED SOMETHING.

WE DON'T CHALK UP NO LS WE BURN THEM.

I NESTLE THE BELL RING IT IN THE MORNING.

YOU HUSTLE FOR REAL YOU GETTING WITH THE GOING?

SEALING EVERY DEAL NOW I'M SWIMMING WITH THE DAUPHINS.

YOUNG HAWKINS YOU BRAVE AND YOU BOSTON?

I MEAN BOSSY YOU FLOSSY DON'T CROSS ME.

I DO THIS OFTEN BIG TEN ALL SPEED.

PEDDLE TO THE GOLD, THANK GLITTER FOR THE GLORY.

IF GAME WAS EVER SOLD THIS MY TRUE STORY.

I DUMB IT DOWN NOW IT WILL SOUND REAL WHORING.

SKEET SKIRT SKEET SKIRCH THIRST TRAP FLOW.

PICK A LAME LINE AND MAKE A HOT GIRL SONG.

I JUST PICK UP WHERE I LEFT OFF I'M NEVER GOING WRONG.

QUICK TO STEP OFF OF A ONE MAN THRONE.

FLOWATREE

COLORFUL JOURNEYS OF A BUTTAFLY

DREAM WORK WORKS, TEAM JERK EM WRONG.

JUST LOWER OUR TAX AND YA EYE BROW BONE. ~

THREE POINT FIELD GOAL IN THE PAINT OR THE GRASS.

I GO SWISH LIKE A THREE FOR THE MATH.

UP HIGH DOWN LOW, YES I GOT SWAG.

I BE BLOWING ON DICE, CEE LO OR THE CRAPS.

I BE ROLLING ALL NIGHT ALL THIS CASH IN MY BAGS.

I TURN A ONE NIGHT STAND, INTO A DOWN ASS DAD.

I DO IT FOR THE KIDS. MOVING DRAMA TO THE PAST.

OH MY LLAMA I'M SPITTING LIKE A BIG MOUTH BASS.

I'M GOING TO LET IT SHINE EVERYWHERE I GO.

IN THE MIRROR LOOKING PRETTY YUP THERE WE GLOW.

FEBREZING ALL DUMB SHIT WE CAN CLEAR ALL SMOKE.

JUST DON'T EASE UP ON ME WRONG BECAUSE THIS QUEEN IS STILL BOLD.

REALLY WATCH YA MOUTH AND PROTECT YA NECK.

TEAM LOVE WE COME THRU WITH AN EXTRA SET.

ALL MY BLOODS BLEED BLUE WE GOT THAT PURPLE DRIP.

MY KIDS REFRIGERATOR ART GOT ACCOUNTS AND SHIT.

IF YOU DON'T FINISH WHAT YOU START IT MIGHT AMOUNT TO GRITS.

BUTTA BISCUITS CHEESE EGGS AND A WELSHER SIP.

OR A OJ GULP CONCENTRATED WITH PULP.

MISSIONS OF SOME KINGS AND QUEENS IN A LAND OF THOUGHTS. ~

BOUGHT SOME LA GEARS AND HUNG EM UP ON THE LINE.
PUT MY CLEATS ON MY FEET HUT HUT GAME TIME.

YOU CAN'T TELL ME I DON'T SHINE WATCH YA BLIND SIDE.

HEAVEN MARY AND A GUCCI SAC, FIRST DIME.

STILL TAKE A KNEE, I'LL KAEPERNICK WHILE YOU DODGE.

REMIND THEM ABOUT THIS TOP, THANKS FOR THE LONG DRIVE.

HEAD ON THE HIGHWAY, HIGHWAY HIT I PLEA, TONGUE TIED.

FORGIVE ME FOR THE TRUTH IF YOU ARE PLAYING

GOD.

I JUST PLAYED AN INSTRUMENTAL, I'M GUILTY I KILLED ANOTHER RHYME.

PULL YOUR SKIRT UP CHERRY FROM THE SIDELINE.

ALLEY OOP TO A TOUCHDOWN.

I AM A FIELD MINE.

DAK DASH ON THAT ASS SHOW YOU HOW THAT COOP RIDE.

I SMASH THEN PASS TO MY LEFT AND RIGHT SIDE.

UNTIL MY MOMMY RICH I'MA LOVE BLESSING MINE. ~

FLOWATREE

COLORFUL JOURNEYS OF A BUTTAFLY

HEY WHA GWAN?

I PON DE RIVER THEN I ROLL UP ONE.

SPECIAL DELIVERY EVERY TIME I COME.

CAME THRU HE KNOCKED OFF MY SOCKS AND MY BUNZ.

EDGES GOT A LITTLE MESSY BUT I STILL HAD FUN.

HASTA MANANA I GOTTA CATCH THIS RUN.

GOT THEM SECOND QUESTION GUESSING LIKE WHERE SHE FROM?

SEE I CROSSED THE BORDER LIKE A CHAMPION.

NO LAW AND ORDER OR A VICTIM WHEN MY TEAM IS DONE.

COMMON TATER TOTS TEST IT WAS A GOOD RUN.

NEW SEASON AND NEW AND ONES.

THE SAME REASON I MADE THIS BIG THREE ANTHEM.

BRING THE BALLERS OUT, YES BALLIN IS BACK.

WHO CAN SHOOT A FOUR WITH ALL NET?

ICE CUBE GREW POINSETTIA NOW POINTS ARE SET.

TELL YA VISION YOUR CHANNELING THE VERY BEST.

RUNNING ALL RACES, DIBS ON ALL TRACKS.

HURRY UP AND WIN, BRING THAT CHIP BACK.

MEDDLE TO YA CHEST.

GOLD RIBBONS LIKE A CHIN STRAP.

YES I SMELL SUCCESS BUT WHERE THE CENTS AT?

I CAN'T FAIL, WE DID NOT EVENT THAT.

YOU GOT MAIL, LOL GET IT BACK.

SMACK THAT, WHIP IT, RUB IT DOWN, FLIP THAT.

TITTY ROCK YOU TO SLEEP, KID NAP.

POP OUT AT THE LOKE, GIFT WRAPPED.

IN THE MIDDLE OF THE CAKE, ALL ASS!

CAN'T GET IN THE PARTY WITH A HALL PASS.

GO SHIT WHERE IT'S GREENER GET YA OWN GRASS.

MAKE GOOD WITH MY PLACE I DON'T KNOW LAST.

THRU ANY HOOD, I'M SAFE PRO SWAG.

SHOOT GUN THE WRATH, COOP OR DA JAG.

MAKE SURE MY LOUIE NAB A CHICK BAG.

WNBA OFF GLASS.

DOUBLE DRIBBLE IN THE PAINT, MY BAD.

TEST ME AIN'T NOTHING SLOW I'LL PASS.

DON'T RUSH ME, IT GETS WETTER WHEN I GAG.

I KNOW WHAT I'M DOING I BRING LIFE TO YA BALLS
BACK.

FROM THE FIELD TO THE TRAP IT'S THE SAME SAC.

WE CAME FROM OUR MOTHERS AND WE ALL GOING
BACK.

BACK TO THE LAND WHERE WE ARE BLACK.

I FEEL A SECOND HUSBAND, WHERE HE AT?

ARE YOU REGISTERED? GET THE STRAP. ~

FLOWATREE

COLORFUL JOURNEYS OF A BUTTAFLY

I RIP AND I RHYME, I RHYME AND I RIP.

ON AND OFF THE COURT LIKE D. L'S. WRIST.

HYDRAULICS WHEN I SPIT UP AND DOWN WITH THE LIBS.

PLEASE KEEP IT HALF FULL ON THE ROCKS I LIVE.

I BOX FOR THE PACKAGE, REFUEL OFF THE GASSING.

WE BRING A MULE WITH A MASK IN.

I ANSWER THEIR ASKING'S.

NO LIMIT THRU THE TRAFFIC.

GET MY ROLL ON AND BACK FLIPS.

N.O. TO A YES MAN I'M NOT WITH THEM QUESTIONS.

EAST COAST TO WEST POINT I'M SMOKING THE BEST FRIEND.

BLESSED A FEW HEROES, I LOVE ALL MY EX MEN.

SKIRT CURVE WEIRDOS, PEACE AND BLESSINGS.

MARY HAD A GYRO EXTRA SAUCE AND A PEPSI.

I AIN'T TOO PROUD TO BUTTA UP THE SCRAPS THAT THEY LEFT ME.

AT LEAST I KNOW THE MILL GOOD BON APPETIT CHECK PLEASE.

I FINGER WAVE TO SHOW THESE KIDS HOW A JET SPEED.

SALT LIFE, SPRINKLE A LITTLE PEP IN THE STEPPING.

A MILE A MIN TO THE NATIONS OF DESTIN.

ANY CROWD WE IN IT, YELLING BLACK IN ACTION.

I'M SITTING WITH THE REAL CALL IT SATISFACTION.

LOVE LIVE AND A LOTS OF LAUGHING.

PRAISE THE POWER, FUEL OUR SOUL OF PASSION.

AGE AND DESIRE, STILL I ROSE.

HA, NEWBORNS IMMORTAL FLOWS.

LUKE WARM I GOT THE CODES.

CORN FIELDS OF GOLD.

I SWEAR ON MY SHAE COTTON PICKING TOES. ~

PEEP GAME I KEEP THAT G GRIP.

ALWAYS STARTING SO IT WILL BE SHIT.

JUST GO HARD UNTIL YOU REACH IT.

DON'T ENTERTAIN THE HATE OR LEECHES.

KNOW YOU RIGHT GOT THEM SCREAMING FROM THE BLEACHERS.

ALL WHITE DON'T STEP ON MY SNEAKERS.

ANY UPTOWN ALL THE WAY TO EGYPT.

SURROUND ROUND SOUND, I THINK I HEAR PEOPLE.

SEVEN SENSES KEEP THE OTHER THREE THO.

TENNESSEE KEEP IT TIGHT WITH ME HOE.

WE FINNA TO SEE HOW FAR WE GO.

A NEVER ENDING MARATHON SEQUEL.

I'M SCREAMING HOLA HOVITO.

THAT'S WHAT I SAY TO MY BIG BRO.

HE SAY SAY KEEP THAT, LA KEY LOW.

STEEL FACE, YOU KNOW HOW WE DO.

FUCK IT UP, FIX IT, FLIP IT.

LOCK IT DOWN, HOLD IT HIGH THEN KISS IT.

FLOWATREE

COLORFUL JOURNEYS OF A BUTTAFLY

GOD MADE DIRT WATCH ME REMIX IT.

EASY WORK MY WRIST JUST FLICKING.

MY PINKIE RING STILL SHINING.

LOVE TO ALL THE BLOOD DIAMONDS.

NEW RELATIONS ALL THIS FINE GRINDING.

REVELATIONS I'M NOT LYING.

IN DO TIME WIN AMEN. ~

SO MUCH GAME IN THE GAME.

I JUST SCORE IN THE PAINT.

HYDRO PLANE THROUGH THE RAIN.

LADY COUGAR GREAT DANE.

SO AMAZING NO PAIN.

ACHIEVING FINANCIAL GAIN.

RELIEF WHEN MY KIDS BLING.

THRU STEAM I BE VENTING.

SO SORRY BUT I MEANT IT.

THE MORE I SMOKE THE BIGGER THE PHILLY GETS.

BOUCHER WITH THE BLOCK IF I AIN'T FEELING IT.

TOUCHE WITH THE HITS I BEEN LIVIN IT.

STILL PRAY FOR ALL MY NIGGAS DEALING IT.

LIKE A DEALERSHIP, I CAN FOREIGN WHIP A FLIP.

REBORN AGAIN, GOD BODY IN THIS BISH.

BODY ODY ODY ODY ON GOD I'M SUPER RICH.~

Author's Note

I have been in love with writing lyrics and making music for many years. I pray that my passion for flowatree and the deeply rooted sound continues to grow. The ability to creatively merge sentences to make a unique sound is a gift from God. The thought of performing on stage in front of millions gives me butterflies out of this world. Holding on to all of my God-given talents doesn't make me feel any better either. With massive material, I decided to sit in my thoughts and create a book. I know it will sound so cliche, but I am truly "sorry for the wait." Music is my first love. I am so grateful and I honor my hip-hop brothers and sisters, my R&B queens, divas, and the men of soul. I pray for the success of all Black artists. I am proud to stand beside those legends who came before me and expressively tell a vision. I put together this book to create a wave avenue of positive vibration for my lyrics. An inner voice for my readers to express themselves and spirituality while exploring colorful journeys. Rap literature is a relaxing way to still enjoy hip-hop music with an induced sound. Flow is a rhythmic wave that leads to an ongoing pocket-catching thing. May you all be upright in heart as you flow through the chapters in this book. I want each reader to enjoy my hip-hop on a new academic inspirational level. There is also some economic information for us to grow generational wealth as one nation. God bless and thank you all.

About The Author

An artist and creative writer with a distinctive smooth style, Taushae Barber, also known as Shae Buttafly, is a child of God from Harrisburg, Pennsylvania, a mother of two, and more to come, God willing. In 2021, Taushae Barber founded *ButtaflyInk International LLC, a 3D, multimedia, writing, and distribution company. This woman/minority-owned corporation focuses on educational scholarships, musical arts, sports science, and Black culture analytics. Taushae has designed platforms of intellectual property, intending to raise capital and create distribution channels for people like her to have protection and security in and outside of their communities. This amazing author is currently in the process of creating a book sequel for her journeys. Ms. Barber uses her platforms to promote change, talk about activism, and advocate for minorities, women, and children while moving with a purpose. She has been working inside of community organizations and public/private agencies within the high-profit/nonprofits and energy sectors. She is grateful for her space and prays her work continues for years to come.*

FLOW LIKE A BUTTERFLY
STING LIKE A BEE.

www.ingramcontent.com/pod-product-compliance
Lightning Source LLC
Chambersburg PA
CBHW071603120726
47973CB00043B/37